WHAT LOVE
MADE
POSSIBLE

A Memoir of Healing
from Intergenerational
Complex Trauma

CHRISTINA GRAHAM

First published by Ultimate World Publishing 2026

ISBN

Paperback: 978-1-923255-77-7
Ebook: 978-1-923255-78-4

Cover design: Ultimate World Publishing
Layout and typesetting: Ultimate World Publishing
Editor: Vanessa McKay
Image Copyright: Invato Design-Shutterstock.com

Ultimate World Publishing
Diamond Creek,
Victoria Australia 3089
www.writeabook.com.au

-TESTIMONIALS-

"Deeply moving, powerful, and at times sassy, 'What Love Made Possible' is an outstanding Australian debut about healing from childhood trauma.

As the daughter of a Vietnam vet growing up in a time where children were expected to be 'seen and not heard,' Christina experienced things no child should ever go through. And yet, she refused to let it destroy her.

Having heard hundreds of stories over the years from trauma survivors, I can say with full sincerity that this book moved me profoundly. Christina's courage and ability to balance harrowing truths with grace and strength, is a skill many writers never fully achieve, and I know this book will help many on their journeys of healing and freedom. Read this book, you won't regret it."

Jas Rawlinson,
Best-Selling Author, Award-Winning Speaker
and Survivor

Christina is a pillar of hope, a creator of change. Her incredible bravery and courage is inspiring. Her story is inspiring. She is inspiring. This beautifully written memoir is both confronting and liberating and it truly shows what love can make possible.

Gemma Cullen,
Personal Development Facilitator

My dear Christina, what an emotional journey this was for me to simply read your story and revisit the therapeutic moments we shared. Thank you for the privilege of sharing this journey. You have taught me much and I am humbled by your courage.

Joseph Riordan,
Clinical Psychologist

It's wonderful. Your honesty is refreshing and your way with words as always is captivating.

Rebecca Thompson
Therapist, Spiritual Mentor and Musician

-DEDICATIONS-

To my husband Ricky. Thank you for showing me what it feels like to be loved exactly as I am. You are a very special person, and I hope I get to marry you again in every lifetime to come.

To my beautiful children Joshua and Grace. It's my life's greatest joy to hear you call me mum. It's a privilege to be your mother and I'm sorry that I haven't always got it right.

And lastly to my sisters, Narelle and Jacqueline. I'm so sorry that we didn't get the parents and childhood we should have, if I had three wishes I'd share them with you.

-Content Warning-

My Dear Reader,

Please observe that this book contains discussions about domestic violence, child abuse, school bullying and a stillbirth. I have written these sections as sensitively as possible to give the reader insight into my experiences and what I overcame. I provide plenty of cues for what is coming so you can decide for yourself if you want to read those parts or not.

It is important that I honour my story and myself by not minimising my experiences, but I appreciate some may find this content confronting, so I ask that you exercise your discretion.

Contents

-Authors Note-

This book has bounced around in my head for a very long time. Part of the difficulty in writing it was I'd been trained to never tell. *What happens in the family stays in the family*, echoed in my brain every time I thought about telling my story. I also lacked confidence in myself. When I'd think of writing it, I'd wonder who would want to read about my life? Being seen and heard has always been uncomfortable for me. I thought someone else's memoir would be infinitely better or more interesting than my own. The other difficulty was the story didn't have an ending. It was still unfolding and changing and taking on new and sudden surprises. On the 19th of March 2020, an end of sorts came, and the story took shape and came into focus.

I finally made up my mind to put pen to paper laying alone in a hotel room in Townsville, having just dealt with my dad's estate in the beginning of the COVID-19 pandemic. Everything was systematically shutting down around me, and 1,400km from home, I faced the constant daily threat of being shut down in a hotel room with no food. Most of it was written in my head during the subsequent two-day drive from Townsville to Jimboomba bouncing down the Bruce Highway in a Kia Picanto.

Laying exhausted on my hotel bed looking up at the ceiling unable to sleep, what I had achieved not only in the past two and a half days, but my entire life came into focus. I began thinking about it and marvelled at my life. I stopped downplaying the significance of both my achievements and barriers. As I lay there wondering if this hotel room was my new home for the next three months, I felt proud. *Genuine pride*, not just a that a girl kind of pride, but *chest swelling* pride. This was hard to deal with as a 50-something woman. For a woman of my era, it was almost a cardinal sin to have any type of self-pride. You are conditioned to be humble, to put others ahead of yourself. Your needs come last to everyone else. So, laying there feeling prideful surprised me enormously.

I began realising how much of my life today had been shaped by my experiences and the decisions I had made. Some of those experiences were sad, difficult, and scary, but others had been beautiful, loving and life changing, and I was grateful for all of it, the good and the bad. I began realising I'd lived two different lives. One as a child and then as a woman. Both entirely different, but each one forming a part of my life that would influence my future and create unique and profound life experiences that taught me lessons in resilience, love, and healing.

It's not been an easy life, but who can honestly say they've had an easy life. Everyone's life has its challenges. Our power is in how we respond to them. How we use these challenges not only to help ourselves but those around us. I don't want my story to be a sad story about a little girl who grew up surrounded by violence and poverty. Though I did. I want my story to be about how strong you can be, how sometimes the people who you thought were the demons aren't and how life through the eyes of a child is so very different through the eyes of an adult. I want this story to show what's possible when you shelve preconceived expectations, and you open your mind. When you can forgive and love the person standing in front of you exactly as they are and no matter what the odds, you can achieve incredible things and that the decision is yours and yours alone.

If this story is never read by anyone other than me because I chickened out and I didn't go further, then that's alright too – because this is my story and my choice who I decide to share it with; just as yours is. So, if you're reading this, then go me, I finally did it.

-THE ARMY-

Boom! The sound of the giant gun echoed through the air, ricochetting off the surrounding buildings and grandstand; bouncing back so we could hear it a second and third time as it faded into the distance. The smell of gunpowder hung in the air as the grey blue smoke drifted out of the spent cartridge that lay discarded at the soldier's feet and hung thick in the air like creepy fog in a horror movie. The smell reminded me of cracker night. Snuggled up under a blanket watching drunk adults recklessly run around the streets with lit crackers yelling, "Hey watch this," at the top of their lungs. Fun hit differently in the '70s. The cheering of the crowd masked the cries of startled children who weren't used to this display of firepower, but I was. I stood proudly on the side of the parade ground smiling widely as my dad's unit had won again. Pulling apart a howitzer gun, which looked like a cannon on wheels, running the full length of the parade ground and putting it back together was my dad's speciality, and he was the best in Australia at it.

In that moment, he was my hero and all other aspects of our lives faded away. He was the dad I wanted, the dad I needed. He was strong and brave and had fought for our country, and I was furiously proud of that. I stood and watched as my dad's unit effortlessly dragged the reassembled gun along the parade ground, smiling and waving to the crowd as they went. Australia's best and brightest trotted out to the public to arouse a sense of patriotism and wonder and maybe inspire others to join up of their own free will, since conscription had been abolished in 1972 by the Whitlam Government. The army had taken a big hit from the bad press of the Vietnam War and recruitment stayed in full swing in the years after. On reflection I now realise it was the whole family being used as part of the advertising campaign, as wives and kids sat around adoring their soldier dads and husbands, embracing, and smiling at the end of the display as if sending teenagers off to war had no impact on them whatsoever and that they came back to be happy family men. Nothing could have been further from the truth.

Before my first trip to Townsville, I lived in the western suburbs of Sydney with my younger sister Narelle. She is 16 months younger than me. We moved around a bit due to mum and dad regularly breaking up and reconciling. I remember living in Canley Vale, Cabramatta, Liverpool, Lethbridge Park, and Holsworthy all before the age of eight. For as long as I can remember, I knew Dad was in the army. It was a massive part of our existence. To this day when I picture him, it's hard to imagine him in civilian clothing. The image I see is dad in his greens, shiny black boots, a green bucket hat and a heavy canvas green belt with brass clips. When I was older, I was taught how to polish and shine elements of his uniform. The rising sun from his slouch hat is still imprinted on my brain.

Mum had many jobs, but rarely kept them for more than a few months.

When they were separated, mum would often leave us with people for prolonged periods of time. Sometimes it was with cousins or friends, but mostly it was with our Granny and Granda. I absolutely loved it when I was left with my grandparents. I always felt so happy and safe being in a place where I knew I was wanted. A weekend visit would often spread out to a month or two, with mum unable or unwilling to be our mother. Dad avoided his responsibilities too by volunteering to do army work that often took him away from home for weeks and months at a time.

My granny and granda lived in a housing commission estate in Lethbridge Park. Many Scottish migrants lived nearby, and I was fortunate enough to live in a community that had little but what they had was shared generously and with great hospitality. We spent so much time within the Scottish Community I famously started school with a Glaswegian accent. I still pronounce certain words with a slight accent from time to time. I was a tiny little girl, freckled faced, with bright curly red hair that flopped about my head unable to be tamed. That's the Irish in you, my granny would say, proud of her mixed heritage. My sister was smaller again, a tiny blonde child with beautiful big blue eyes, timid from what she'd already witnessed. Two little girls who went everywhere together. My granny, Sarah Wilson and my uncle Joseph Martin were the founders of Lethbridge Rangers Soccer Club, which would become known as Mt. Druitt Town. They and my granda, George Wilson are life members there and you can still see their names at the club to this day. Whilst Mt. Druitt Town is a big deal these days, back in the 1970s it was just a paddock and a red brick toilet block, where I spent a lot of time running around and cheering from the sidelines. Ladies would meet on a Friday night at my granny's house, and each bring a bag of potatoes. They would sit around solving the problems of the world and gossiping, all the while cutting up chips that they'd deep fry on the weekend at soccer games inside an old army tent which served as a makeshift canteen. No food handling laws in those days.

I have no recollection of any type of violence during this time, though there was. My days were filled with going to school, watching Skippy the Bush Kangaroo, with the Wonderful World of Disney on the weekends and Countdown on a Sunday night. Snuggling up on my bed and being embraced by my oversized Holly Hobby rag doll whilst reading baby animal books was my most favourite thing to do. I dreamt of being a vet and saving all the animals of the world, holding the realities of my family life at arm's length, safe on Holly Hobbies lap. My grandmother has since told me there was violence and a lot of it to the point, she had offered to adopt us so mum could go and live her life. Sadly, mum refused to give us up, permanently anyway. Unfortunately, it was the worst thing my granny could have done as the next time mum wanted to leave us somewhere it was not with her.

-Don't Tell-

My first recollection of physical violence was during one of the times my parents were separated. I was about six or seven years old. Early one morning I found my mum crawling on her hands and knees being sick on the floor of our tiny flat in Canley Vale. I was really frightened and wondered what was wrong with her. We didn't have a phone, so I went and got a neighbour to come and help her. When I brought them back to the flat, Mum was standing on her feet, looking like nothing had happened at all. After convincing the neighbour she was fine, and I was nothing but a little busy body they left. With the door barely closed and without warning, my mother spun around and hit me so hard across the face that my teeth felt like they were going to come out and were loose in my head. Searing pain radiated throughout my jaw and my ear burned. I instantly felt sick and white lights pulsed behind my eyes. The momentum of the blow she landed unbalanced my very drunk mother, and she fell into the wall, causing her to fly into a fury.

"Who the fuck do you think you are?!" she hissed inches from my face, stale beer and lemonade on her breath.

"I knew it was a mistake having you. You're nothing but trouble," she continued, her finger wagging in my face.

"You don't ever tell anyone anything that happens in this house ever again!" she spat, spittle flying everywhere, landing in my hair and on my face.

She grabbed a handful of my hair and dragged me to the bedroom I shared with my sister, slamming the door violently behind her as she left me laying there crying, broken hearted. In my little girl's heart and mind, I had thought I was helping; I thought she was dying; but instead, I had accidentally outed her for the drunk she was. She was embarrassed and ashamed and wholeheartedly took it out on me and I couldn't understand why. The next day, she told us to pack our bags. We were going on a holiday.

-Two Little Girls-

My sister and I were so excited to be going on a holiday as we had never had one before. I can't remember exactly what I packed, but I remember packing a class photo from Canley Vale Public school. I have very few school photos, perhaps because of the expense of them, our frequent moving, or a lack of my parents being bothered, so this photo is especially precious to me to this day. When I was little, I used to pretend the teacher in the photo was my mother. Her name was Mrs. Worthington and when I felt sad, I would sleep with her picture under my pillow. Somehow, having my teacher there made me feel safer. She was so loving, and kind and I felt at peace knowing she was close by. She had a way of making me feel like I was the only person in her class, and she was there just for me. I wanted to be just like her when I grew up.

We owned an old, brown Valiant Regal and my sister, and I loved sliding into each other all over the back seat. However, this day, Mum made us put our seatbelts on. It was a very hot day, and my legs began sweating on the vinyl. I asked Mum if we could put the radio on, but she refused. We drove in painful silence. The trip was very long and boring and Mum didn't speak to us once the whole way, so we were very relieved and excited when we finally got there. We eagerly got our bags out of the boot, and it was then I realised mum didn't have one. It began to dawn on me what was happening, remembering the routine of all the times we'd been left somewhere before.

"Where's your bag Mum?!" I asked with apprehension.

Without looking at me she shrugged her shoulders and replied, "Oh, I must have left it at home. I'll get you girls settled in and I'll go back home to get it and come back later."

She never came back. My mother drove off and left her two little girls five and six at a children's home, telling us we were having a holiday. My sister stood screaming on the front step whilst a stranger dressed in grey tried to stop her running off after Mum's car as it slowly became a dot in the distance. I just stood there with my little brown cardboard case still in my hand, wishing with all my heart I had never told our neighbour about my mum. As the dust settled on the road, I began thinking if she ever came back, I would never ask for help or tell anyone anything again.

My sister and I were taken to a small office. The biggest fish tank I'd ever seen was pushed up against the wall. The harsh florescent light that sat over the top made the goldfish in it glisten and look more cheerful than the surroundings we were in. The light shone on the top of my sister's hair forming a halo and her beautiful blonde locks were hanging forward over her face. I could tell by her slumped shoulders and bowed head she was still crying and refused to look up. I went to her and held her in my arms, full of guilt, as this was all my fault.

The large office chair was big enough for two little girls to sit side by side and I comforted her the best I could. My family had always told me I was the oldest and my sister was my responsibility, so it was up to me to keep her safe. As I held my baby sister in my arms, I could smell Mum's shampoo in her hair and the thought of being at home made me feel sad, but I caught myself before I started crying. It was my job now to look after my sister, I thought, and big girls don't cry. After what felt like an eternity, a faceless lady finally came to get us. She silently led us to a dormitory full of bunk beds. They lined the floor as far as the eye could see, with just enough room to pass between each one. White iron frames standing cold and uninviting, housing unwanted children under grey woollen blankets that itched and smelled like damp socks. At the end of the hall was a wall of blue dented lockers, mine was 16 and I put my case in without unpacking. If I didn't unpack, it meant I wouldn't be staying here. On the first night my sister and I slept together, holding on to each other under the scratchy grey blanket. My photo of Mrs. Worthington tucked neatly under my pillow.

I don't know how long Narelle and I were there, and I still don't know where *there* was. We were in some type of children's home, and it was for a long enough period that we attended school, were seen by a dentist and got new clothes, so I imagine it must have been some time. Long enough to think this was my new home and long enough to forget my old one. I don't have a lot of memories of this place except visits to the sea, singing Mr. Bojangles in a bus and lying awake at night wondering if my mother was ever going to come back for us. My little suitcase remained unpacked in locker 16, eagerly waiting her return.

I was in class one day, and the faceless lady finally came to get me. She took me to the office we'd first arrived at; my sister was already there. The big fish tank, unchanged except for the light that didn't seem to be on this time. Our little brown suitcases were standing neatly next to each other on the floor. My heart skipped a beat. Were we going home? No one told us anything, adults didn't in those days. It was as if children weren't smart enough to know what was going on or not important enough to be informed of adult decisions. My sister's head shot up when she heard me come in and I joined her on an old orange settee and moved us both back into the corner. I never took my eyes off the door.

It wasn't long before the door of the office flew open with such force it banged into the wall behind it, and I couldn't believe my eyes. Our granny burst into the room, looking around frantically, calling out, "Where are my grandchildren?"

Before anyone could answer, she spotted us sitting on the old settee and she swooped on us like a seagull on a chip. I'll never forget how happy I felt that day being smothered in her ample bosom and her landing kisses on our heads like we were being pecked by Woody Woodpecker. We were going home, and I didn't even care that we didn't get to say goodbye.

When I grew up, I tried to find out where Mum had left us, researching children's and girls' homes in the 1970s but most are closed now, the records long gone. When I brought up being left later in life, no one in the family would share what happened, where we went, or why we were there. Shame and secrecy cuts deep and leaves wounds that are hard to heal. I can't imagine what was so bad that could have made my mother leave her two little girls in the care of strangers. I can only imagine, but for me it taught me never to tell. My first attempt at getting help had been an abject disaster. When I told, when I had tried to get help, I got sent away and punished and so had my sister. That was how it felt and in the absence of any explanation from the adults in my life, it was the only conclusion I could come to.

-Holsworthy-

Life returned to normal for a while. There was always a honeymoon period when Mum and Dad got back together. They momentarily seemed to forget all the reasons they had parted in the first place and got lost in the euphoria of their regained love. Dad had secured a married quarters house as part of his posting to Holsworthy Barracks. We lived on Sanananda Road. I was so proud of myself that I had learned how to spell it overnight. It was a sweet little house across the road from a swing park and walking distance from our school and a swimming pool. Our school had mainly army brats attend it and every morning we would have parade, standing at attention and then at ease whilst the flag was raised. We'd sing *'God Save the Queen'* and walk in neat quiet lines to our classrooms where our hands and nails would be checked for cleanliness before we were admitted for entry. Above the blackboard was a sepia portrait of our young Queen and a faded map of the world hung on a board at the back. We'd finish each day by reciting The Lord's Prayer before placing our little wooden chairs on top of our little wooden desks. To get to school, we'd cut across the fields dodging the magpies in springtime. It was around this time I could feel the love I had in me. My kindness and compassion touched everything I said and did. I would befriend the kid at school that no one liked, bring home stray animals and nurse them to wellness. To me, it seemed more logical and natural to treat others with loving kindness. It felt good to be this way. I cared deeply about the world and everything in it.

I was fascinated by nature and the world around me, spending hours escaping into the school library reading books about baby animals, the weather and digging through The Encyclopedia Britanica, heavy voluminous books so expensive you weren't allowed to borrow them. By the time we moved to Holsworthy, I knew there was something wrong with my parents, in the same way that I knew something was wrong with a sick animal that I'd adopt and nurse back to health. I didn't know what it was, but I could see they weren't like other adults I knew. I feared and loved them in equal measure. Their behaviour was unpredictable and frightening. Several years of living in a volatile environment were starting to fine tune my survival skills. Being able to read a situation quickly would become a vital skill that would mean the difference between life and death. My well-developed powers of empathy were refined trauma responses born from hypervigilance and, whilst extremely useful, would also create so much stress and confusion for me. Knowing there's pain going on for a person but being too young to know what to do with that information is torturous. Empathy is both a blessing and a curse, especially when you're only eight.

In the 1970s the second wave of feminism had arrived in Australia, not that you would have known it in our house. '*I Am Women, Hear Me Roar*' was not being played on our radio. I was a little girl, and I hated being one. I didn't get to do half the fun things I saw boys do. I remember getting into big trouble at school one day for 'showing' the boys my underwear. I was hanging upside down from the monkey bars at little lunch in my school uniform – a dress, unbecoming behaviour for a girl, with plenty, ready to tattle on me the minute we got back to class. As a result, I was put over my dad's knee and belted with his army belt, the brass clips cutting into my knuckles in my feeble attempt to fight off his assault.

"Don't. Show. Boys. Your. Underpants!" he bellowed with every blow felled on my tiny behind.

In his attempt to teach me modesty, he crushed my trust in him instead. I couldn't see a single thing wrong with what I had done. *Why hadn't the boys gotten in trouble for looking?* I thought, not daring to say it out loud.

I loved visiting my cousin's house. My uncle, Mum's brother, lived in Holsworthy too and had two boys. Playing with them was great fun as they had trucks, cars, building blocks, Lego and balls to play with. They also had swings. At our house we didn't have many toys. What we had was a training ground to be good little mothers and wives. Baby dolls, tea sets, prams and nurse dress up sets made for tedious play afternoons. I felt it wasn't fair that boys got to have more fun than I did. I wanted to be a vet or teacher when I grew up and I didn't want to have a baby. I had a whole different life planned out for myself, but 1977 had different ideas about what little girls should do and that got me in a bit of trouble.

I was such a curious child that it took a lot to keep me occupied. We had no books in the house and the only library I could access was the schools, and that was closed most of the time. I would read what I borrowed quickly so that would often leave me with little to do. To keep myself amused, I would make up stories, often pretending that they were my life so I could escape what was fast becoming a very toxic family situation. My name would always be Lucinda, my sister's Mary, and we would convince other kids in the neighbourhood we were just visiting from Scotland on a magnificent holiday as our parents had died. We would tell them we had come to visit with our aunt and uncle in Australia who were considering adopting us. The last remnants of my Scottish accent helped to sell the story. I'm not exactly sure how my parents found this out. I suspect my sister accidentally told them, but as you can imagine, they were not amused to find out they were dead and replaced by someone else. The punishment was harsh. I still carry the scars on the back of my hand and hip from it. The punishment had been for telling lies. Ironically, telling lies was something I learned from my mother when she sent me to the door to tell the Waltons man she wasn't home. It was okay to tell lies when it suited them. It was a do as I say, not do as I do kind of house.

Telling stories after that became a private affair and one, I kept only for my sisters. I'd use the stories to distract them from the violence going on around us, taking them down a rabbit hole of fantasy and fairies where it was safe, and no one could hurt us. It took many years before I'd share stories publicly again, until then they remained unspoken in my head. It feels so good to be getting them out and into the light now where they belong.

The Christmas of 1977 would be our last in New South Wales. I didn't know we were moving to Queensland the following January. Parents didn't tell children things like that then; you had no say in anything and just went wherever you were told to. Dad had been promoted to Sargent and part of his promotion was a posting to Townsville. The town he had trained in and shipped out of when he was sent to Vietnam in 1967.

-Baby Sisters and Ashtrays-

My parents weren't always difficult to be with. Sometimes they could be really loving and happy but that came with its own set of problems. Looking back, I wonder if it would have been easier if they had just been difficult all the time. Then I would have known where I stood and could have prepared accordingly. The problem with parents like mine was you never knew when the switch would flick. One minute you could be having fun, laughing, and playing, the next you would be back-handed and sent flying. What was acceptable behaviour one day wouldn't be the next. It created an atmosphere of constant stress and anxiety and turned me into a people pleaser. If I could just be good enough, I could keep them happy and then they might leave me alone. Mum had changed a bit since she'd left us and didn't hit me as much anymore, but she would often make cruel comments about how I looked or how stupid I was, always making sure she would rain on any happiness I tried to create. Despite this, I have happy memories. Things were especially good when dad was away with the army. Some of my favourite memories are of us sharing toasted cheese sandwiches very late at night.

Sitting up in Mum's bed watching silly late-night horror shows in black and white. Obviously fake vampires dramatically biting into someone's neck or *The Blob* growing and engulfing someone's town. When Dad was away, I always became Mum's best buddy, having fun and hearing secrets little girls probably shouldn't be hearing. It was sad that she lacked a friend to confide in, but it wasn't surprising considering her mental health problems. Her only companion was her eight-year-old daughter. It was on a night like this that I heard Mum was expecting a baby. I was going to have a baby sister, I hoped, and I was absolutely thrilled. A new person in my world to love. The idea of it gave me so much joy. I instantly started thinking a baby in the house might help them stop fighting.

When Dad got home from army exercises, the atmosphere was always much more tense. Things were a little more rigid and edgy and mum was always much harder on us. It was during one of his home comings that I'd get some insight into why Mum was the way she was. We had spent the night as a family, eating a meal and watching tv together. It was such a novelty to have Dad home, so my sister and I sat eagerly on the floor next to his chair, one either side of him waiting a direction. Our job as children was basically to do all the menial errands your parents didn't want to do, so a prod in your backside and a glance at an empty beer glass would indicate, *go and grab Dad more beer.* You might be needed to change the tv channel, adjust the aerial for a clearer picture, empty an ashtray or even brush your parent's hair, but being useful was a great feeling and I did it without complaint.

Our bedtime came, we gave our parents a peck on the cheek, said good night and took ourselves off to bed. I was awoken from a deep sleep to a loud crash. Something was breaking, and my mother's yelling pierced through the darkness. It wasn't the first time my parents had fought, it was a regular thing, but this was the first time I remember it being this violent. As I was growing older, more was coming into my awareness. They barked the most impossibly cruel things at each other. Dad began claiming the baby wasn't his and Mum, fully enraged by this accusation, began throwing things at him. Household items were crashing and breaking all over the floor. Enraged by the insult, my mother lost all sense of self preservation, so when she called a returned Vietnam Veteran a baby killer, all hell broke loose. Everyone in 1970s Australia knew what a profound insult that was. Even as a child, I knew that was a very bad thing to say and terror began flooding my veins. Sitting bolt upright in my bed, I could feel bile rising in my throat in anticipation of what I knew was going to happen. The air in the house felt electrified with rage and I could feel it metres away.

Our house in Holsworthy was only small and going by the debris field I cleaned up later, I assumed after Mum's comment that she'd made a run for it through the kitchen to get out the back door. Dad had caught her at the stove just before making it into the laundry, which was towards the back of the kitchen. A pot of soup bones had been simmering on the stove hours earlier and she'd hit Dad in the head with it, spraying the walls and refrigerator with ham soup. I was frozen in my bed, terrified to make a sound and hoping my sister in the other room was doing the same and that's when I heard it. A gargled sound was coming from the kitchen. It sounded like someone trying to breathe and speak but they couldn't. Then there was frantic banging on the kitchen door. It scared me, but I could feel there was something wrong.

Without hesitation I decided to get out of my bed and check that everyone was ok. I was terrified as I opened my bedroom door. The banging was getting louder and more frantic, and my heart began thumping harder and jumped into my throat. I walked slowly down our short hallway into the lounge room. The coffee table was upturned, ash and cigarette butts strewn over the floor. A broken ashtray lay in pieces at the bottom of the front door. The TV had a hole smashed into the front of it and Dad's chair was lying on its side. Mum's chihuahua Pebbles was sitting under the lounge enjoying the spoils of war, trying to chew on a ham bone three times her size that she had managed to salvage without being trampled to death by my parents as they fought. My mum and dad were not in the room. I realised the noise I could hear was coming from the kitchen, so I made my way carefully around the corner. What I saw chilled me to my bones.

Dad had Mum against the door, both hands around her throat. Her face was turning purple, and she was kicking the door, trying to get away. Dad's head was bleeding heavily, and a small pool of blood was forming on the floor.

"Dad!" I screamed at the top of my lungs, "Stop it! You're hurting her!"

He instantly let Mum go, her visibly pregnant belly heaving as she tried sucking in all the air she could. As we stood there staring at each other, my dad began moving towards me. I began bracing, as I was sure I was going to be next. Instead, he pushed me aside and walked slowly out the front door. Mum fell to her knees, the soup wetting the edge of her floral cotton nighty. She put her head in her hands and began to weep and shake all over. Standing next to her, I hugged her tightly, her head coming to rest on my chest. As her tears eased, she looked up at me, black mascara streaks down her cheeks; her black teardrops had reached the top of her nighty and had come to a stop.

"He's going to kill us one of these days", she whispered. "He's going to kill us."

As she calmed down, I helped her to her feet. Holding her hand, I walked her to her bedroom and went back to the kitchen to make a cup of tea. She shouldn't have called Dad a 'baby killer', but I knew she hadn't deserved what I had witnessed in our family kitchen. I locked and chained the front door and, using the wedge that would usually keep the back door open, I kicked it under the closed door to jam it shut.

He wouldn't be killing us tonight.

-Welcome to Townsville-

The first trip to Townsville that I can remember was in 1978. There had been another earlier one, but I have no living memory of it except recounts from Mum and Dad of driving from Sydney to Townsville. They'd taken the trip in a Holden station wagon with a mattress in the back for my sister and me to sleep on.

My dad was a professional soldier. He had joined the Australian Army at 19 so he could be part of the Vietnam Campaign. His family had a proud history of serving King and Country, so for him it made logical sense he would follow in their footsteps. Having arrived in Australia in 1959 as a 12-year-old, 10-pound pom (though the Scottish didn't take the term 'Pom' kindly), his displacement from his proud Scottish culture and a sense of kin and community served even more strongly to push him toward service, doing something familiar and helping him connect and bond with his newly-adopted country.

As a result of Dad's military career, my childhood was disrupted. My dad was extremely intelligent – bordering on gifted and his skills and experience were very much sought after. He was an artilleryman- no one could pull apart and reassemble a howitzer more quickly than his squad could, and I was always so proud when he'd win the competitions, and his gun would fire first. He and his squadron featured in the army recruitment adds on TV and in the papers in the '80s. He was a soldier in demand.

We had been living in Holsworthy married quarters with dad stationed at the Barracks there but in the '70s it dawned on the Australian government that keeping all their active soldiers primarily in bases in Melbourne and Sydney would be a tactical mistake. So, we were posted to Townsville.

We arrived in Townsville on an extremely hot and steamy Thursday afternoon on the 19th of January. I had been heartbroken to go, I was nearly nine and my younger sister seven, and we knew no one. Our family life was extremely volatile at this stage- a returned Vietnam Veteran with 797 days in combat and very bad PTSD and a mother of dubious mental health herself made for a very toxic dynamic. At least in Sydney, we had family. We stayed regularly with our grandparents. We were engaged with the Scottish Community through gatherings, soccer, parties and get togethers, but up here we were alone, no buffers and no one to run to.

My fear was temporarily negated by two events. First, I flew on a plane for the first time. In the 1970s, this was very special, as only rich people flew in planes then and rarely children. I remember my granny taking my sister and I shopping for some good clothes to wear for the journey, as in those days such travel required your Sunday best. We were the only children on the flight and the Ansett Air hostesses fussed and made a big deal over us, which was exciting. What I realise now as an adult was the hostesses were fussing, because my mum was heavily pregnant. Full term, in fact. How she got permission to fly I will never know. My granny used to say that Mum could *charm the pants off a priest* and seeing as we were about to fly to Townsville, I'd say there was someone sitting in their underpants somewhere. The belt couldn't be fastened properly over her huge girth, and the hostesses were rightly on edge. This brings me to the second event. Mum was about to have a baby.

There is almost 10 years between me and my youngest sister. My parents had desperately been trying for years to have another child after Dad returned from Vietnam. With two girls they were hoping for a boy. After Dad's first tour of Vietnam, my sister Narelle had been easily conceived in the backseat of a Holden at someone's party; it was 1969, Australia was at war and Dad was heading back for a second tour. I was already in existence from a previous relationship, and after violence in that relationship, Mum had already moved on. Their 'fling' in the Holden was meant to be a one-night stand. For Dad, he instantly fell in love, as Mum was a beauty. She could have been a model, she was smart and sassy and had a red-headed temper that could have put the incredible hulk to shame, and he fell hard. Sadly, there have never been two people who were more poorly suited for each other than they were.

Dad stayed an extra tour in Vietnam doing three in total, being seconded to the Americans for his expertise in communication and artillery. He came back to a beautiful blonde baby girl, taking me on too as one of his own, a ready-made family, but they wanted one more. After being exposed to agent orange, amongst other things, conception took a while and the pregnancy came as a big surprise as Mum and Dad had given up trying, even separating because of it. Finally,in 1977, Mum discovered she was pregnant, and I was going to be a big sister and couldn't wait.

Dad had flown to Townsville a week prior to get everything ready for our arrival. He met us at the airport where we had to walk across the tarmac to get to the arrivals area. I could feel the heat burning up through my shiny new black shoes, the soles had slightly melted. I could feel them grabbing and squelching as I walked, entirely inappropriate footwear for tropical north Queensland in January. The airport was cheerless and unwelcoming and seemed to be full of army personnel coming and going or standing around smoking and laughing loudly. I didn't especially want to be here and wished with all my heart I could turn around and hide on the plane so it could take me safely back home to my grandparents in Sydney.

"Hurry up, we're parked in a no standing zone," was Dad's greeting, as he rushed us towards the baggage area.

By this stage, Mum's walk had slowed somewhat and she stopped at regular intervals to catch her breath. Completely oblivious to what was happening, Dad yelled, "Hurry up!" again.

After collecting what little luggage we had, we made our way out of the airport. Parked immediately outside the door was an army Jeep.

My heavily pregnant Mum, who by now knew she had gone into labour, took one look at the Jeep and groaned, "I don't bloody think so!"

Laughing, Dad said, "All good Trish, the Jeep is for me, you and the girls are going to go in that one," pointing to an army car parked closely behind. A sheepish looking soldier at the wheel gave us a small wave whilst dad bundled us into the back seat, leaving mum to hang onto the passenger door, straining and panting, trying to catch her breath.

"Just follow me," he ordered the young chauffeur of our car, the house is about 15 minutes from here. Waiting a moment for mum to get into the front seat, he then jumped in the jeep, and we dutifully followed behind.

Now that I am a grown woman who's been married for almost 30 years I have a full and complete understanding of the different ways that men and women think and behave, I cherish and love these differences, however as a child I did not - so when dad said he was going to Townsville to get our house ready I fully expected to arrive at a readied house. All I can say is yes, there was a house.

The armed forces had built a suburb of military married quarters for the families coming from down south, they were cyclone proof high set concrete bunkers with interwoven tiles and cyclone fences all designed to make us feel like moving to the tropics wasn't going to kill us. In those days when the army transferred family's interstate, nothing came with you. We had a suitcase with a couple of personal items, but everything else we owned went into storage. The army provided a brand new, fully furnished three-bedroom family home. Quite the sales pitch. When we pulled up to the house in Aitkenvale, we could barely see it for the ridiculously long grass. I didn't even know grass could grow that big. It was so long that Dad's Jeep disappeared into it. Unamused, Mum turned to the driver and said curtly, "Go back to the airport now," he laughed and said, "It's ok mam, they all look like that at first", and pulled up to the curb.

Dad excitedly rushed to our car, machete in hand. "Give me a second," he said. "I'll just cut the grass off the path so we can go upstairs."

I heard my mother exhale deeply. We finally arrived at the front door of our new house, only to see army issue furniture had been dumped quite literally into the first room they found; it looked as though someone had backed up a tip truck and tipped a three-bedroom house full of furniture into the lounge room.

Now I suspect my mum had been in labour on the plane and this sight did nothing to calm her. Her labour pains became more obvious as she waddled around the house, surveying the scene. After several moments of silence, Mum decided that a quick grocery shop was in need and left the house, ordering the young soldier to take us to the local shops. I was never privy to the conversation that passed between Mum and Dad before we went to pick up some supplies, as we got the go wait in the car command- but when we returned most of the scant furniture supplied stood in its rightful place, with a very sweaty and red-faced Dad greeting us at the roadside when we got back.

By this stage, Mum's labour was quite advanced so my sister and I were dispatched quickly from the car with bags of shopping and told we will see you later. As I stood with my sister on the side of the road, I wondered what hell I had arrived in. I was hot, tired and hungry and my parents had just left us standing in front of a jungle. Welcome to Townsville.

-Narelle, Jacqueline and Family Dinner-

It was over a week before we got to meet our baby sister. In 1978 the niceties of having family around a new baby hadn't eventuated yet and siblings were viewed as germ carriers from hell and to be kept away from babies at all costs, so when we went to visit mum in hospital the best we got was sitting on the veranda whilst Dad held our baby sister up to the window to see.

School hadn't started yet and was still out for summer holidays, so we had been left to our own devices whilst Mum was in hospital and Dad at work. Narelle and I had made an intricate maze of paths and cubby nooks in the very, very long grass in our back yard. I'm not even going to try and think about what would have been living in there. Now when I say grass I mean what we had in the backyard was definitely a member of the grass family in the same way that sugar cane is- it reached up through the hills hoist and could cut you if you moved through incorrectly – when the army finally arranged a tractor slasher to come in and cut it the guy mowing had to stand up in the tractor so he didn't hit the fence just to be able to see.

Whilst this bit of fun had provided a distraction, being completely separated from all our family members as young children was not ideal. My sister and I slept in the same bed for the first few weeks, telling stories and singing songs to entertain and comfort each other. At that stage in Townsville, the TV didn't start until the afternoon and mostly covered local North Queensland news, The Sullivan's and Australian News- we couldn't even watch the shows we had enjoyed on TV in Sydney and had no toys to speak of. It was another familiar thing removed and another thing to mourn.

Our baby sister was eventually named Jacqueline; she came home from hospital in a cane basinet on the backseat of the car with a seatbelt wrapped around her. A far cry from bringing my first babe home from hospital where I virtually had to produce a certificate from the ambulance station stating the baby capsule had been put in my car by a trained professional before I could leave the premises.

The first few months of living in Townsville started to fall into a routine. We finally got enrolled in school and walked the 2km alone each way, whilst Mum was busy with the baby. I was totally besotted with my little sister and spent every waking moment tending to her, playing with her, feeding her, I pretended she was mine- my own Baby Alive doll. Playing with my baby dolls had never been this much fun. My sister Narelle wasn't as thrilled as I was. She had been the baby of the family for several years and had been cruelly demoted and she wasn't taking it laying down. At any opportunity she could, she would do something to make the baby cry. A photo being taken, the baby would be screaming as Narelle would be squeezing her hand behind our mothers back, laying outside in the sun, the baby would be screaming as Narelle would be pinching her toes, laying asleep, Narelle would yell in the room and wake her up- a sad little girl who just needed some attention and boy was she about to get it.

There had been no incidents since we had arrived in Townsville, Mum and Dad had been on their best behaviour and I thought moving to Townsville and the new baby had fixed everything; I was very, very wrong. The first incident that signalled how wrong I was, came one evening when baby Jacqueline was about six weeks old. We were all together sitting eating dinner. Dad was very specific with his army routine and dinner had to be on the table no later than 1800 hours, 6pm if you're a civilian. My sister Narelle was a fussy eater and fiddled a lot with her plate and food, she wasn't quite eight yet and trying to manage the adult sized cutlery provided by the army, was proving challenging. The way she was eating her food started to get on dad's nerves.

I knew the signs well and a cold chill raced from my head to my toes, my body became fully alert and bolt upright waiting for what action I'd need to take and then it happened. My sister, still struggling with her cutlery trying to cut up the meat on her plate, scraped the knife or fork across the top of the plate making a high-pitched noise that I can only equate to nails down a chalk board. Mum and Dad had seen the poor kid struggling all mealtime – she just needed a hand, someone to cut her food for her, but instead she got a backhand from Dad that snapped her head so far back that the back of her head hit the back of the chair. Dad jumped to his feet, sending his chair flying and threw his plate which exploded inn pieces all over the wall. I dove under the table just in time to see the pieces bouncing to the ground, instinctively covering my head. From my vantage point all I could see was my sisters' legs disappear straight up from under the table kicking away. I don't know how he grabbed her, but as he dragged her up the hallway to her room, her flailing legs collected the baby's basinet which crashed to the ground. My mother began wailing and crawled towards the screaming baby that had toppled out and Dad unbuckled his army belt. They disappeared out of sight into my sister's room, but I could clearly hear the punishment she was receiving. Mum sat cross-legged on the polished wooden floor, crying, cradling the baby in her arms, whilst Narelle screamed louder with every landing of Dad's belt. I crawled out and started quickly picking up the pieces on the floor worried what might happen if he emerged, and the mess was still there. I made myself scarce for the rest of the night laying awake and wondering how my sister was. I went to school the next day, she didn't. It would be my turn another day.

Domestic violence and child abuse were not things people talked about during this time. To be honest we barely talk about it now. So, a week or so away from school wasn't uncommon for us to hide whatever injuries had been inflicted. A black eye here, a broken nose there, explained away with a few days at home and a note to the teacher describing what current mishap had caused this month's injury. If anyone suspected anything we never knew it. People 'politely' minded their own business, and we were trained never to speak outside of the home. Family business stayed inside the family. No help lines, no internet, no phone. Just a day-by-day struggle to survive never knowing when the next incident would come, never knowing who'd be attacked next; it was exhausting. Home was never a place you could relax or let your guard down. Fortunately for me I lived in Townsville and the outdoors was all mine.

-Dingoes, Mangoes, and Fruit Bats-

Townsville as a child was such a magical place to escape to and explore. After living in the built-up city areas of Sydney, Townsville was like another planet. Animals and plants I'd only ever read about or seen in books existed here and I wasted no time exploring every creek, river, cave and rock pool I could find. When I was out exploring, I felt safe and calm. Being in nature was and still is, incredibly healing and soothing for me. One benefit of having inattentive parents was they really did not care where we went, how we got there, what we did or who we were with, as long as we were home by five o'clock. If we got our jobs done around the house and stayed out of our parent's way, the world was ours.

Wild fruit trees grew along the banks of the Ross River. Bananas and paw paw grew everywhere and were handy for a quick meal and saved having to go home to eat; not that there was always food there. Trees laden with mangoes hung over onto the footpaths and could be eaten by anyone going by. Huge monstrous trees so big they could almost cover a whole backyard. I can still smell the rotting fruit, so abundant that it had fallen on to the road, squashed by cars. The large stone in the centre flattened out, drying in the sun. A mosaic of mango seed tiles filled the road from one side to the other. When they weren't in fruit, they were marvellous to climb. Near every tree there would always be some poor fruit bat strung between the power lines, electrocuted before they reached their delicious mango treats. Eventually, a wing would break off and they would fall to the ground. The bat carcasses lay in wait on the footpath for hordes of kids with sticks to poke at or pick up and throw at other kids, who would run off screaming down the street. My sister and I would often make bets to see how many days it would take to fall. Whoever lost would have to wash AND dry the dishes. The natural beauty around me at least gave me respite from the ugliness of life at home.

When people talk about their most precious childhood memories, I often hear them speak about their family, or birthday parties, holidays, or special events. I don't have any of that. My precious childhood memories are of trying to tame the 'dingo' that lived at the bottom of Mt. Stuart or sitting on the banks of Ross River making daisy chains and pretending I was the River Queen, and the flowers were my crown. Jumping off the bridge and trying to touch the bottom of the river or going down to The Strand to see what interesting things might have washed up onto the beach. I have some precious memories of how much I loved my sisters, but mostly my best and most favourite memories were just me, my pink Malvern Star push bike with a little white basket on the front exploring Townsville.

Dad was everything you would expect from a Sargent in the army. Your bed had to be made a certain way, our clothing always neat and tidy, manners always and mealtimes strictly adhered to, no exceptions. When he was away and Mum was left alone though, things got a little looser and freer.

"When Dad's away the mice will play," Mum would sing, immediately getting out her hidden bottle of Bacardi before Dad's car was even around the corner. Mum's drink of choice was Bacardi and Coke, or a shandy if money was tight. I'd often get sent down to the local shops with an empty Coke bottle in my little white basket as payment to pick up more Coke and cigarettes. A handwritten note was all that was required for a child to buy their parents a packet of Winfields; my reward was cashing in the empty Coke bottle for 20 cents. Dad frequently left on army training and called it 'going bush', so when he went bush, the fun would begin.

Mum really preferred to be friends with us, rather than mother us. I suspect making friends with her peers was too taxing, or they asked too many questions. She often felt more like my irresponsible older sister than my mother, so it wouldn't be unusual for her to 'go bush' herself sometimes and leave me alone with my sisters for the weekend. Without my grandmother around for accountability, it became a free for all. I'd stand on a chair to cook food, or we'd just eat left over rations from Dad's previous bush exercises. I'd pretend the house was mine and my sisters were my children. I'd dress them up and ride them around the neighbourhood, Narelle on the handlebars and my one-year-old sister between my legs balancing precariously on the edge of the long bike seat. No helmets, no shoes. My granny always said there are special angels who take care of children and all I can say is I must have had them in the truckload. It is an absolute bloody miracle my sisters and I made it to adulthood. The thought of my kids riding around the neighbourhood on a bike at that age with no one at home to miss them chills me to my bones, but in Townsville in 1979, no one blinked.

-Family Secrets-

It was on return from one of Dad's exercises that I'd find out that my dad wasn't my biological father. I had always assumed Dad was my dad. In hindsight, there were some obvious genetic indications that he wasn't but what nine-year-old girl understands that. Mum wore a wedding band, and everyone called them Mr. and Mrs. Martin. We were the Martin family, and no one had ever indicated to me otherwise.

Dad had been away for three months on exercise. It was the strangest thing, that even though he scared me and made our home unsafe, I still missed him like crazy when he was gone. Abused kids still love their parents, and I loved mine. My sisters and I had been counting down the days for his return. We had drawn pictures and made cards that had 'Greatest Dad in the World' scrawled in wobbly cursive across the front, accompanied by a stick figure in army greens holding a gun. Being the over achiever I am, I even made a little banner that I stuck up on the dining room wall. *Welcome Home Daddy,* it happily declared. I was so proud of my work and began to bathe myself in my father's imagined gratitude of receiving it. I played out the scenario in my head of my dad wearily climbing the front stairs weighed down by his huge backpack, walking into the house and being thrilled by what his little girls had made him. I imagined being taken up into his arms and being hugged and kissed. In my imaginary world, he may even have said, *I missed you.*

He'd been sent to Hawaii to do more training, and I had put up with three months of my mother's resentment at having been stuck in 'boring' Townsville with the kids while he was away.

Her less than subtle barbs of, "If I hadn't had you lot, I'd be in Hawaii right now," got old fast so Dad coming home was a welcome relief, despite his unpredictable behaviour.

We waited and waited all afternoon, and our excitement faded to disappointment when he didn't show up. With no phone in the house, he had no way to contact us, but this didn't stop Mum going on a rampage about what a useless human being he was and how utterly fed up she was at being stuck with ungrateful kids all the time. Just what every kid wants to hear. As darkness started to fall, she decided we would all go out and buy take away for dinner, a rare treat that renewed our excitement immediately.

When we got home, the house lights were on, we knew Dad was home. We were so excited we jumped out of the car before it barely stopped. I took the stairs two at a time in a rush to get to him. I'm unsure if I was excited to see him or just excited for him to see my cards and banner, but either way, I burst into the room full of girlhood enthusiasm eager to greet our long-absent parent. Dad was sitting at the dining room table, my lovingly made *Welcome Home* banner waving gently in the breeze just above his head. I could tell immediately he was drunk, very drunk and looked tired and annoyed.

"Where the fuck have you been?" he barked at me. "It's passed five o'clock." I froze in my tracks.

At that moment, Mum walked through the door, carrying Jacqueline who was just starting to walk but far too little to manage the stairs on her own. On her heel was Narelle who was carrying the dinner; fish and chips nearly as big as her wrapped up in newspaper, the steam transferring yesterday's news onto her forearms and chin. In an echo of Dad's words spoken seconds before, Mum looked him straight in the eye and said curtly, "And where the fuck have *you* been?"

Without taking her eyes from him, she handed me the baby and took the package of food from my sister and started unwrapping it onto the table, her silence demanding an answer. As the tension between them grew, I could feel myself desperate to break it. In my little girls head, I thought now would be the perfect time to give Dad the cards we'd worked so hard on and ushered my sisters into my room to retrieve them. By the time I got back, plates had been placed at our seats and Dad was drinking straight from a large bottle of VB. I enthusiastically approached him, brimming with love and yearning to give him the welcome home I'd imagined in my head, still hanging onto the hope that he'd see my card and return to a happier state.

Mum continued busily setting the table whilst I handed him my card. As I stood there, smiling waiting patiently for the praise and love I believed was coming my way, Dad dropped the card on the table like it was on fire and my heart froze. I could smell the beer on his breath as he heaved a heavy sigh of aggravation in my direction. Completely confused I just stood within striking distance staring.

Finally, he spoke, "You must really be the stupidest kid I've ever met," he spat viciously in my direction, "I'm not even your father," he said coldly.

"Jim!" Mum screamed, "Now's not the time for that!"

She did not deny his statement.

Dad leapt aggressively to his feet, knocking the chair to the floor in the process,

"So when is going to be a good time, Trish?" he hissed in her face.

I could feel my heart painfully breaking in my chest, and I let the other two cards we made fall to the ground. My parents flew into a full-blown rage, trading insults and accusations, until Dad grabbed Mum by the throat and slammed her into the wall vibrating the house. I didn't intervene like I had in Holsworthy; still reeling from the news of my parentage so cruelly delivered that I didn't know what to do. Mum managed to spit in his face and the shock of it made dad slightly loosen his grip. Relief began flooding my body until he made a fist and threw a punch.

I squeezed my eyes shut not wanting to see it delivered. Instead of the crunching of bones I heard the cracking of fibro and wood. Dad had punched the wall close to Mum's ear, breaking his hand. He let her go and walked out the back door, still dressed in full army greens. Seeing her chance, Mum hurriedly snatched up the baby and rushed off to her room. Narelle had already disappeared. I was left standing alone in the dining room. I looked at the broken wall, my banner still hanging in place, trying to summon some type of normalcy or happiness but failing. I picked up my cards and threw them in the bin and went to my room, leaving the fish and chips to go cold on the table. I wasn't hungry anymore and just wanted to go to sleep. My welcome home party was destroyed, and I didn't know who I was anymore.

Like everything else in our family, Dad not being my dad wasn't brought up again. The next day, it was like nothing had happened. Apart from a round fist sized hole in the wall no physical evidence remained of the evening before, wiped from the room but not from my memories. I began to think it was just a mean thing that he'd said. Maybe somewhere deep down he wished he wasn't my dad and I think that thought was worse.

-Tippy Toeing-

It wasn't all bike riding and beaches in Townsville. I also had school. As nature was my sanctuary, so was school. It always had been. It was a place I got a break and felt safe. I idolised my teachers and used to imagine them adopting me and taking me home. School was easy for me. I could read for as long as I could remember and loved the challenge of learning new things, so any time I got hurt at home and I had to have time off, it upset me deeply. I hated missing school. I attended Aitkenvale State School, and it was there I decided I was going to be a teacher when I grew up.

School in the '70s and '80s was a lot different to what it is today. Shoes were optional. Everyone either walked or rode their bike to school and we had little brown cardboard suitcases we called ports we'd carry our lunches in. Usually, devon and tomato sauce sandwiches on pay week that would peter out to Vegemite by the end of the fortnight. They were loosely wrapped in greaseproof paper and presented to us in brown paper lunch bags. The lunch bags also doubled as book covers at the start of the year. We all had drink bottles with a lid on that became a cup. It was usually frozen and wrapped in a tea towel, so we had something cold to drink with our lunch. We got inspected for head lice, went home if it got over 40 degrees and learned our times tables by rote. Teachers could give out the cane and throw dusters, but it was nothing compared to what went on at home. I knew if I was a 'good girl' at school, I would be safe.

I loved everything about school and the games I played at home with my sisters often involved me setting up little classrooms and reading aloud to toys who were co-operative and excellent students. Due to my homelife, I had developed into a very mature and responsible child for my age, so I often got to do special jobs for the teachers as I finished all my work before everyone else. My self-worth became linked to how I could be of help to others. My favourite job was helping make the stencils. Purple work sheets that everyone would sniff as they got handed out around the classroom. School gave me a sense of routine and security; it was predictable, and I was very good at it. My parents were never interested in my academic achievements, they were never in the room when I got an award, I never got to attend school camps or excursions, mum didn't attend my school graduations, but I didn't care. I liked that they didn't come into this part of my life. It gave me freedom and joy. Well, that was the story I told myself to ease the disappointment of their absence. Outside of my sisters, school gave me a sense of achievement and somewhere to go.

The longer we stayed in Townsville the more my dad seemed to unravel. Every time he returned from an exercise, the more sensitive he was. He would disappear into the sergeant's mess for hours on end, often returning drunk and abusive.

He gambled and smoked, leaving us short on money. We'd frequently go to school without lunch and eat baked beans on toast for dinner. In public, Mum and Dad put on quite a show. Loving on each other like newlyweds. It was so confusing watching them. Mum would laugh at all his dumb jokes, touching his arm, "Oh Jim," she'd coo. Dad would buy her a drink and bring it back to her, planting a kiss on the cheek, "This is for you sweetheart," then they'd look lovingly into each other's eyes. It was worse than 'Mrs. Bucket' on *Keeping Up Appearances*. Dad was the sergeant and Mum the sergeant's wife and keeping up appearances was everything to them. He oversaw a platoon of lower ranked soldiers helping train them in the ways of the army. He couldn't be teaching discipline and control to soldiers if his own family didn't present the same.

I think, after a while, Dad couldn't find the line between what was work and what was home, treating our family like an extension of his platoon, creating rules and routines that only seemed to make sense to him. Discipline in the army is very important. Their lives could literally depend on it, so rule infractions were dealt with harshly. That also applied in our home. Dad saw us as tiny green soldiers who should follow and remember every single rule. I was always living in fear. My sister Narelle was the worst rule breaker in the house. She was younger than me and would just forget things getting herself in trouble time and again. There were so many injuries occurring in our house I became excellent at first aid. I borrowed books from the library so I could figure out how to stop bleeding, how to treat burns and the best ways to treat a concussion.

Being helpful and knowing what to do made me feel special and important. Our family violence was so normal I had contingency plans upon contingency plans for when the worst occurred. I had skilfully figured out that if I took everyone into my bedroom and pushed my bed between the dresser and the door, it jammed the door shut, Dad couldn't get into the room and would eventually lose interest and leave us alone. I turned surviving into some type of game show, leveling up after each incident when I'd discover something I'd forgotten. Eventually my room became fully equipped with towels to stem bleeding, snacks in the drawers and a bucket in the wardrobe for vomiting or the toilet, whichever came first. My sisters and I spent many hours hauled up in my room, sometimes with Mum and sometimes without, hiding until the coast was clear and we could come out again.

Mum and Dad were going through a good patch. Mum was pregnant with her fourth baby and Dad hadn't been on exercises for quite a while. It felt good to be a family at times like this. Dinners ran smoothly. We went to school every day. Yard work was done. We'd watch TV together as a family. It lulled me into a false sense of security, and I let my guard down. I've always drank gallons of water, even at night, which often means a trip to the bathroom. On such a night, I sleepily awoke to answer the call of nature. I was closest to the toilet and literally had to turn a sharp right from my bedroom door, and I was right there. After finishing up, I tip toed out, only to be ambushed from behind. I could feel cold metal pressing at my throat and a strong arm was wrapped around my chest pinning my arms to my side. The deep growling voice of a man whispered in my ear.

"Who the fuck are you?"

Before I could answer he repeated, "Who the fuck are you?" pressing harder at my throat and giving me a shake.

The words were very breathy. I couldn't recognise the voice. I could feel the man trembling behind me as he pulled me closer in. I could feel his heart thumping into my back.

"I'm not going to ask you again you little fucker. Who are you and what are you doing here? I swear to God I'll slit your throat if you don't tell me now!"

Everything happened so quickly and so slowly. My head was swirling. No amount of clever thinking was going to help me here, so I froze like an animal being hunted. I stayed quiet, calm, and completely still. My feet fully rooted to the floor. Hot breath on my ear, cold metal at my throat. Somewhere in the distance, I heard my parents' bedroom door opening and my mother's voice burst through the darkness.

"No Jim!" she screamed with all her might, desperation in her voice. "It's Christina, let her go!"

I felt his grip loosen and heard a metallic clang on the wooden floor. Looking down, I could see my father's machete laying at my feet. Loud crying filled the air; behind me, my dad had collapsed on the floor. He repeated, "I didn't know it was you; I didn't know it was you; I didn't know it was you", cradling his head in his hands, rocking backwards and forwards whilst he knelt on the floor.

Too shocked to speak, I looked up from my crying dad and met the eyes of my mother. They were wide and terrified. I'd never seen my dad cry before and stepped away from him, feeling sad and frightened all at once.

"Go to bed now!" she ordered, and I did, closing the door behind me. I heard her pick the machete up and walk down the hallway. A cupboard door opened, then slammed shut. My father's cries eventually stopped, and then there was silence. I lay in my bed checking myself for injuries. There were none. Relieved, I hugged myself, rocking gently back and forth, and stroked my hair until I fell asleep.

When I woke the next morning, Dad was gone. "He's away bush," was all Mum said, but I knew it was a lie because his backpack was still at home. After that night, he never laid a hand on me again.

-Baby Andrew and Sad Goodbyes-

I was a lot less excited about the second baby that was coming. Another person to look after and worry about in my world just felt too much. Dad constantly kept telling everyone how he hoped this one was a boy, "Fourth times a charm," he'd grin, making me wonder why girls weren't as important.

Mum was also less excited, "What am I going to do with another baby?" she complained to me, explaining how the three kids she had already were holding her back from the life she'd dreamt of. I think sometimes she forgot I was one of the kids she complained about, and I didn't know what I was supposed to do with information like that. I felt sad that Mum didn't have the fun she thought she should have, so I tried my very best to be good and look after my sisters. I thought if she had less to do and we were all perfect children, her life would be more satisfying somehow, and she'd be happier. But the reality of it was that it didn't really matter how much we did, it just never seemed to be enough. Looking back, I can see how that first trip to Townsville entrained me to put everyone ahead of myself. I began prioritising other people's happiness and needs over my own before I was 12 years old. Everyone and everything were more important than me.

As mum came closer and closer to her due date, my responsibilities grew even further. I liked feeling useful and needed but the responsibility was way beyond what any 10-year-old girl should have been shouldering. I had missed out on much of my childhood. Playing with toys was replaced by bathing my sister; playing games was tidying the house and doing laundry. I had less time to explore the beautiful world around me as I tended my ever-expanding mother. I stopped playing and eventually I forgot how to do it all together. One of my great feelings of sadness is I have so few memories of being a free and happy child, enjoying the blissful sweetness of childhood. In a drunken fit once, Dad had revealed there was no Santa or Tooth Fairy when I was six and I had been looking after a baby and a seven-year-old from the age of nine.

Sadly, this last baby would be the beginning of the end for my parents. It's hard to know what happened between them in the end, but the result ended with my baby brother being born sleeping and mum nearly dying in the process of his birth. I felt like I hadn't looked after her well enough and the last bit of spark my dad had for our family faded immediately. Baby Andrew was born and died March 14th, 1980; six weeks before my 11th birthday. I'll never forget his tiny white coffin in the army chapel and my dad cradling it in his arms as he took it out to the hearse. Walking straight passed; his dead eyes looked straight through us. Three living daughters would never be a suitable replacement for his dead son.

In the fallout of Andrew's passing, my Granny came to Townsville. I hadn't seen her for two years, and seeing her walk across the tarmac at the airport made me cry. I was so relieved to have her there. Mum was still in hospital and Dad had been coming home and going straight to his room, barely looking at us as he walked through the house. To have an adult in the house I could rely on was a huge relief. The weeks following Andrew's death had been very difficult and confusing. No one was telling us anything and we were expected to behave as normal, like nothing ever happened. Whilst Granny was with us, life was a little happy again. I felt so guilty that I was loving having her there. She took us for a day trip to Magnetic Island and we drove around in mini-mokes, standing up and hanging off the back as we explored. We'd lived in Townsville for two years but had never visited. I'd only ever seen the island from The Strand and had always dreamed of going there. I remember pulling into Horseshoe Bay for the first time and thinking it was the most beautiful place I'd ever seen in my life and fantasised about how I could stay there. I loved every minute of having our granny in Townsville and feared what would happen when she left. I had felt the tension rising between my parents, but my grandmother's presence had kept a dampener on it.

When the day came that she had to leave, my heart broke wide open. In the six weeks she'd stayed with us, I'd nearly lost my mother, attended a baby's funeral, and had a birthday that had been acknowledged. It had been both the saddest and happiest time of my life, but it had ended. Waving goodbye from our veranda as Dad drove my grandmother to the airport filled me with dread. I knew in my heart what lay ahead for us. With the added layer of loss, it ended up being so much more than I could have imagined. I had considered telling my granny how bad things might get, but my mother's words of "Don't tell" burned deep into my soul. Memories of scratchy blankets in children's homes and beltings flooded back to me, so I kept it to myself.

My parent's relationship lasted nearly two years after losing Andrew, and it went how I expected it to. What parents living like this don't realise is your kids know everything that's going on. They think they can hide it from us, but they can't. When you think your kids are asleep, we are not. We are lying in bed, awakened by the tension in the air, the raised voices, the crashing of furniture and paintings as they're pulled from the walls. We see and hear everything, and it scares us. That's how it was with my parents. Fighting in the darkness with no awareness that their children could hear them. That their children were watching. That their children were being irreparably damaged with every hit, every cruel word, every missed meal, every race run unwitnessed. Parents in title alone. By army terms, they were derelict of their duties. If we had been in the army, they would have been arrested and court marshalled by the same military police who began showing up and taking my dad away for the night, only to bring him back the next day, turning their cheek away from the bruised eyes and broken bones. Just stay out of his way and don't annoy him, we were told by the Army Chaplain brought in for family counselling. Even when those in authority knew they did nothing. That would continue to be my experience at different times when I got the courage to speak up. My cries for help would fall on deaf ears. Child abuse and family violence are taboo. I learned to suffer in silence. I wonder how many kids still do today.

In September 1982, the Army gave us an indulgence flight to go visit our grandparents in Sydney. We hadn't been back since 1978, and I was very excited to go see them and get some respite from home. Mum told us to pack our favourite things but keep it light as we were going on a military Hercules plane and there wasn't much room for personal luggage. I grabbed my school port and packed some clothes, my toy tiger that I slept with, a book to read on the journey, and my picture of Mrs. Worthington. The flight was long and loud. We sat side on with seat belts built for soldiers with backpacks on. It was very nerve racking, and I wondered as we took off if I might fall out of the back of the plane as the loading door was still down. As I watched the ground fall away and Townsville became a spot in the distance, I felt a flood of relief fill my body.

It would be 36 years before I'd step foot in Townsville again. The trip to Sydney became another 'holiday' that turned out not to be, but at least this time, Mum had a suitcase. Going to Sydney had been an escape plan, orchestrated by my grandparents. I never saw my room again. I didn't get to say goodbye to my friends. I missed out on my softball grand final, but I was finally safe, back home with my grandparents, whom I'd missed with all my heart.

-Girls in the 1980s-

Returning to the western suburbs of Sydney from North Queensland without a transition was hard work. As a 13-year-old in Townsville, I had been in primary school, but in New South Wales, 13-year-olds in grade seven went to high school. So, two weeks after our arrival, I found myself dealing with a school full of high schoolers in Shalvey and school stopped being the haven it had always been. There were fights every lunch time, drug deals in the toilets and a bomb scare every Friday afternoon so the students would be sent home early. I didn't know what had hit me.

Girls wore a ridiculous light pink uniform, reminding us we were girls and the only electives I could choose were home economics and textiles and design. I'd written technical drawing, but someone in the office thought otherwise. Again, my teachers were my saving grace noticing the intelligence I had and providing extra classes in their own time, as learning was frequently disrupted by fights or students jumping out the windows. My end of year report card saw me topping every class, and I'd start year eight grouped in the top classes where learning was slightly less disrupted.

Shalvey was no place for a girl like me. My bright red hair, freckles and glasses were a magnet for bullies. Each day, they tried to wear me down with insults and violence. They'd call me rusty, carrots or red head match, anything but my name. Books and learning were my only friends. By year nine, my science teacher, Mr. Ian Sanders, could really see the talents I had and spoke to my mum about applying for a science program. I'd be able to go into the city once a week and study at a school in there, a scholarship program for gifted and talented students. The idea of getting away from Shalvey once a week sounded like heaven. By 1984, vandals had burned the library and science block down and we were having lessons in sweltering demountable classrooms that circled the school oval. Only about 15 students stayed past year 10, severely limiting the senior subjects I could choose, and I was beginning to worry about my chances of getting into university, so a science scholarship program offered an oasis in the desert.

Several weeks passed before Mr. Sanders called me into the science teachers' staff room. I could see he was angry and annoyed, and I automatically thought it was because of me. I sat very still on the chair, waiting to find out why I'd been called there. Not speaking a word, he handed me an official looking letter; it was addressed to him, but it was about me. It read words to the effect off that because of the high levels of teenage pregnancies at our school and in our district, the department could not justify a scholarship for me to attend the science program in Sydney.

They weren't going to send me because they thought I'd just get pregnant and leave school like so many of the other young women around me. With encouragement like this, who could blame them I thought. Science scholarships were hard enough for girls to get in the 1980s so a girl in my position probably had no chance from the moment the letter was sent in. It never occurred to me that they'd say no, as I knew how dedicated I was, and it took a while for the decision to be fully comprehended.

"It's ok," I said to my teacher, who was clearly more annoyed about it than I was, "I'll figure something out."

"I already have," he said. "We are going to get you into Hurlstone."

Hurlstone Agricultural Highschool is a state run selective high school for gifted students and they only had three positions for enrolment into year 10. It was in Glenfield, which suited me perfectly as my mum and my sisters had just moved to a housing commission house in Ambarvale only a bus and train ride away. I had been staying at my grandparent's place to finish the school year at Shalvey and the idea of changing schools again filled me with dread. I had never heard of Hurlstone, but my teachers had, and they did everything in their power to support my application to attend there. They described the school as a private school that I wouldn't have to pay for and it would provide me with more opportunities for learning as well as a chance to go to university. I only had to put in the work. It was the first time I had an adult believe in me and encourage me and it felt good. I worked and studied every waking minute. Hurlstone was going to be my ticket out.

At the end of 1984, I was one of three students selected to attend Hurlstone. I can't express how much the school meant to me. It gave me a safe haven again. I'd find my first real friend, Veronica. I gained insight into other more healthy ways of living. I was surrounded by people, like me, who loved learning and writing and singing and music and I found out that I wasn't the weird one; that there were others out there like me. To attend a school where learning was celebrated and attendance at university expected made me feel normal because in my family, that sort of thinking made you the black sheep. My education at Hurlstone saved me in so many ways and without it, I wouldn't have the life I have today. I can't express enough how important it is to have access to quality public educational facilities. Maybe if the girls of Shalvey had had that, their prospects might have been more extensive than single parenthood.

As we settled into life in Western Sydney with a single mother, living on a pension in a housing commission estate, our lives didn't turn into sunshine and lollipops like I thought it would.

Mum's deteriorating mental health saw her frequenting bars and the local RSL at Campbelltown, gambling on the pokies and drinking away what meagre amount of money the government spared us. Looking around me, the army life was replaced with the 'houso' life, and I knew this wasn't for me. I wanted something else. My dream of teaching burned hot in my soul, and nothing was going to stop me from getting it.

-For the Love of Teaching-

Good morning Mrs. Graham. I never tired of the way the children in my class sang this to me each morning. Class roll in hand, I let my little charges into the classroom ready for another day of learning. Teaching was everything I hoped it would be, and I could feel a little bit of all the teachers I had loved growing up be part of me as I performed my duties each day. My kindergarten teacher, Mrs. Worthington, was with me when I taught preschool. Channelling her love and devotion to each child as if they were my own. Mr. Thompson, my year seven teacher in Townsville, was with me when I used all the patience I could muster to explain things differently for the 100th time that day. Mr. Sanders, my grade eight science teacher at Shalvey High, was with me every time I told a student to believe in themselves and showed them, they were more than they thought they ever could be. Channelling the words he wrote to me, in a letter, that I carried in my purse for 20 years. I must have read it 1000 times or more. My teachers at Hurlstone who saw gaps in my learning and helped fill them. They knew a good education would allow me to live a different life. Each day I taught, I shared their legacy of teaching and

learning. I knew from experience that great teachers changed students' lives. This was exactly the teacher I set out to be.

After years of disfunction I arrived at my 20s not really having a single clue who I was. I identity farmed traits from those I admired and made them my own. I was a living breathing Frankenstein, but I kept my scars carefully hidden. The reality of me hiding in plain sight, seen but not seen. Lying dormant, waiting to be brought out of the darkness one day. Getting myself to this point in life was hard fought. I'd put myself through high school and university working all sorts of jobs, from selling hotdogs outside night clubs to dressing up like a clown and face painting at shopping centres. I had set my sights on a different life, and nothing had stopped me. I was the first person in my family to finish high school, the first to graduate from university. I had found and married a kind and loving man who's never laid a hand on me or uttered an unkind word. I gave birth to two beautiful children and swore to give them a better life than I ever knew. I wanted their childhood to be magical, beautiful, and long. They never felt the sting of a belt, or the thud of a punch and never went to sleep hungry. I had made it. I had broken the shackles of what was expected from a girl in my neighbourhood. Not only did I survive but I had gone on to thrive. Well, that's the story I told myself. I had honestly thought that I could go on and live a relatively normal life after everything I'd been through, and for a long while I did.

There had been some early signs that things weren't quite right for me. I couldn't cope with loud, busy places. I jumped at loud noises. It was impossible to sit with my back to a door. I could see and hear things other people couldn't, I called them my 'spidey' senses. Social situations gave me anxiety, and I didn't like sudden change. I had plenty of ways of explaining my issues away.

"Oh, thanks for the invite, but I just had a baby."

"Yes, I am very tired, but I am working two jobs."

"No, I didn't sleep last night but the report cards are due."

"No honey I can't go to a movie with you. The kids need to keep to their routine."

I became the Hallmark card for excuses, an explanation for every occasion. Outwardly I looked like I had it all but, on the inside, I just felt dead, and I couldn't figure out why. Having a wonderful family and a job I loved only seemed to heighten the pressure to be happy, but I found myself becoming sadder and sadder. I was acting the role of happy wife and mother and dedicated teacher. I completely and utterly wanted to be those things. It was like all the feelings I had ever felt had been put in a blender and blasted to dust. I just couldn't feel anything, no matter how hard I tried.

Teaching was both the best and worst job for a person like me to have. It gave me structure and predictability which I desperately needed to feel safe, but it also played on my huge need to feel liked and useful. The school system is brutal for teachers who have low self-esteem and no boundaries, and I worked myself to the bone. There was no shortage of bosses, principals and colleagues who encouraged and enabled my people pleasing personality. During my career as a teacher, my people pleasing reached new and dizzying heights, constantly saying yes, when I should have said no, taking on kids that others refused to teach and tasks no one else wanted to do. I was exceptionally good at teaching the hard cases and that made me feel so needed and special for the first time in my life. I loved the kids that fell through the cracks or threw chairs, the ones that thought their lives were going nowhere and they had nothing to lose. I had grown up with kids like that. They had been friends and neighbours. I had been a kid like that, hiding from bullies and barely getting by day to day.

I yearned to be the best teacher I could be. Giving my students the best education possible. I wanted to save every child I could from a life of trauma and disfunction and believed a great education could do that. It had saved me, so why couldn't it save others? A caped crusader for fairness and justice for every child who passed through my room. On reflection, I think a bit of what I was trying to do was save the little girl in me who was starved and bruised. I'd never healed her. I had just pushed her down into the depths of my soul, thinking if I ignored her long enough, she would go away. Like that is even possible. She hung around like a ghost, whispering in my ear whenever she could. I saw her in the eyes of every neglected child. I saw her in every kid that came to school without a lunch. I saw her in every student who missed out on an excursion or camp, and it cut me to the bone. Every second, every day, I ignored her.

Until I couldn't anymore.

-A Perfect Storm-

It was 2007. By then, I'd been teaching for over 10 years. It was such an ordinary run of the mill day with absolutely no hint of what was to come. I was walking my class down to the oval for their PE lesson. As soon as I got there, I was told to take one of my students back to class and lock down with her. A court order had been faxed to the school and family services were on their way to take her and her brothers into their custody. I wasn't to open the door to anyone except the principal and under no circumstances was the child to be given to anyone else. I remember feeling a squeeze in my stomach at the mention of family services. This had been my greatest fear growing up, that someone would take us away from our family and that I might get separated from my sisters. My heart was beating fast, my stomach sat heavy in my abdomen, my student's hand was sweating in mine. This hot sunny afternoon would change everything. A perfect storm of triggering events was brewing on the horizon.

We made our way as fast as we could back to the classroom. In the distance, I could hear a woman's voice screaming out the little girl's name.

"That's my mum," the student said. "She wants me to go to her."

All I knew at this point was that the student was in danger and could not go with anyone other than family services. It was hard to explain that to an eight-year-old as I was rushing back to the classroom, but knowing the mother was now on the school grounds, I ran. With every core of my being, I wanted to protect that little girl, and almost dragged her off her feet behind me.

I blurted, "I just need to keep you safe for now. I'll tell you more when we are in the classroom." And just kept running. Suddenly I couldn't feel the ground beneath me as it fell away. My feet were paddling air, and the world began to swirl.

The mother had spotted us. She was running with a baby in her arms and in her desperation to reach her daughter, tripped. I saw her fall in slow motion as everything in the world around me slowed and almost come to a standstill. There was a loud sickening thud as she and the baby hit the grass; my heart skipped a beat as I saw the baby's head hit the ground. I then froze, my feet planted solid where I stood, the baby's shrieking cry giving way to my heart thudding in my ears. Gasping for breath, I pulled the little girl into me, protecting her from what was to come. Suddenly, I wasn't on the school grounds anymore. I could feel the blows as they landed on my back. I could feel my arms being pulled to get the child away from me, but I held tight, bending over her, protecting her with my body. I wasn't at school any longer. I was back in Townsville. I was holding my sister. I was keeping her safe from my parents.

It was like watching a movie unfold in front of me. I was a mere spectator, powerless to stop it. My wounded little girl had resurfaced. I could see me cradling my sister's body against mine, a mere child myself, both of us vibrating with every blow. I could hear the principal's voice yelling faintly at the end of a tunnel. I yelled back, "Get off us! Why do you have to keep doing this to us?"

The world went black and quiet. I opened my eyes and saw three shocked faces staring at me and bolted for the classroom, locking myself and my student away to safety.

The father had arrived, joining the mother in their quest to retrieve their stolen child. They began yelling through the windows, telling me they'd come back and shoot me if I didn't hand their child over immediately. Finally, the police and family services arrived and took them away, the little girl crying in confusion in my arms. When the knock on the door came and it was time to go, my student looked afraid and asked if I could walk with her down to the car; without any thought I said yes, wanting to keep her safe to the very end.

"What's going to happen?" she asked, her voice quivering, tiny tears building up in her eyes. "I'm sure the lady in the car will let you know honey," was my lame reply. I honestly didn't know what to say, still holding back the shock of the afternoon's events. I walked her to the car and put her in.

"You're going to be okay," I promised, but I felt like I lied. I knew I wouldn't have been okay if someone came and took me away from my family. As the car drove away, she waved out the window to me. In that moment, her face transformed into my sisters. I gasped at the shock of it. As soon as she was out of sight I dropped to my knees and sobbed.

-THERAPY-

"So, Christina, what brings you in today?" Joe, my therapist asked, his kind eyes looking at me with burning sincerity. *Oh god - where to start*, I thought. I had 40 years of life buried deep, aching to make its way into the light.

My experiences of seeking help had never ended well. High school guidance counsellors, well-meaning middle-class people who, in the 1980s, couldn't fully comprehend the extent of mine and my sister's abuse. It was easier to brand me a liar. For people who came from loving families, I'd imagine what I was saying would have been hard to believe. To them it probably sounded like complete and utter nonsense. A story so farfetched that I must have seen it in a movie and taken it on as my own. Labelled a desperate attention seeking teenager and reported to my mother, signalled again some things were just not to be spoken about. My mother was right when she told me that certain things stay in the family. "No one will believe you anyway."

It was a long while before I tried getting help again. That doctor declaring after a five-minute consultation, "You're just depressed; here's some pills. Next."

With pressure building, I'd break down and trauma dump on people. They'd stop speaking to me and who could blame them? I felt ashamed and embarrassed and learned that people don't want to hear these things about you, so my feelings got pushed down deeper and deeper until I couldn't reach them anymore. It was hard to talk with people and have normal relationships. When I'd get to the part of the friendship where you'd be expected to share stories about your life to create trust and intimacy, what are you supposed to do when all your stories are about abuse and trauma? It was so isolating and sad; the tendrils of the past silently reaching through time, continuing in their silent strangulation of the life I wanted to have. Invading everything I tried to build; I was never out of reach.

Casual conversations with other women would turn to reminiscing about their families and childhoods. What are you supposed to talk about when your biggest childhood memory is having a machete held to your throat? It doesn't make for polite morning tea conversation. I built a model of what I thought people wanted me to be. A more socially acceptable caricature of myself. That model involved building up walls to keep people out. A neat little fortress just for me, sitting gloriously untouched right in the middle of it. A fake house for a fake person to live in. Trusting no one, always on alert for when they'd strike and hurt me. I was disbelieved for so long I disbelieved myself. It was easier to survive that way. Let that story belong to somebody else. I left the wounded little girl that was me in the past, holding a story too big to carry alone.

-Confessions-

What brings me to therapy? That question burned in my ears. At the core of it was 20 years of physical and emotional abuse and neglect. I had opportunities to seek therapy before but none of it appealed to me and I couldn't see the point of it. I didn't want to be one of the miserable people sitting around wailing about how sad their lives are. No thanks. My workplace had arranged counselling after being assaulted at school, but I was a very reluctant participant and offended that they had made me go. I was handling it. Therapy was for people with actual problems, not me. I was deep in denial. My parents had been the ones with problems. They had needed therapy. I was strong, I was a survivor, I had my shit together, I didn't need therapy.

So, what finally made me go to therapy?

I had punched my husband in the face.

Writing that now all these years later, it still makes my stomach churn and my heart ache thinking about that day. The shame of it is seared into my soul. I can still see his shocked, hurt face in front of mine like it was yesterday. All he was trying to do was talk with me about my wellbeing, and in that moment – as he reached out for my arm to stop me running away – I lashed out. He wasn't angry; he wasn't being controlling. But fight and flight kicked in, and I ended up in fight.

In the end, I had to face the truth. I had hurt my kind, caring husband, who'd never harmed me. I'd spent the good part of 40 years trying to be the opposite of everything I'd disliked growing up, and in five seconds flat, I undid it all. I went to therapy because I couldn't stand myself anymore. All the hard work, pain and sacrifice I'd made throughout my life felt like it had been for nothing. I'd turned into the very thing I despised and had brought violence into my home, albeit for a moment, but it was five seconds too long.

I didn't teach for too much longer after the incident at school. What had made the situation worse was that there had been no foundation to the accusations. The parents had been wrongly accused. I hadn't been protecting anyone from anything and that triggering event had all been for nothing. From that day on, my love for teaching weakened. I loved the kids, but the system felt increasingly unfair for both me and the students I cared deeply for. More and more was being expected from me as a teacher, with less and less help to do the job. I was tired and burned out. When I first began teaching, it had been such a respected profession, however over the years it was reduced to being judged by test scores and sarcastic jibes about how many holidays you got. I was finding it hard to control my emotions and struggled to cope. When I started spending time in the staff toilets crying almost every day, I knew it was time to take a break, so I took a leave of absence to help my husband establish our Engineering Consultancy which was in its infancy.

My grandparents at this stage were quite elderly and I was enjoying caring for them. We had always shared a close and special relationship, so getting this extra time with them in the twilight of their life was such a privilege. My second application for leave had been to help them after my granny fell and badly cut her leg, nearly losing it to infection and spending three months in the hospital. Caring for my granda in her absence gave me the respite I needed, and at the end of the three months I didn't think I could walk onto a school ground again. Just the thought of it made me feel sick to my stomach. I applied for a longer leave of absence. It wasn't long before the writing was on the wall and a return to teaching was looking highly unlikely. With the engineering business up and going, I needed something of my own to do so I opened a bookshop. My bookshop opened in November 2010, and it changed my life.

-Book Lovers-

I absolutely love how the universe brings the exact right people into your life at exactly the right time. I call them 'angel people'. They always show up when I need them to help guide me where I need to go. I've had teachers in my life like that; some friends during my university years like that and in 2011, two more angels walked through the front door of my shop, just when I was adrift in sadness and didn't know what to do.

I've always struggled with my mental health throughout my life, but after the incident at school it gradually worsened. Even though I had wanted to take leave from teaching, it still crushed me. My entire identity was wrapped up in being a teacher. It was all I had ever wanted to be since I was eight years old. It had gotten me through every difficulty in my life. It had been my saviour; my northern star and I was totally lost without it. I loved my little bookshop, but it wasn't teaching. I won best new business in my first year of operation and putting books into children's hands and promoting literacy in an area with some of the lowest literacy levels in the state was very satisfying, but I was becoming depressed and withdrawn. My husband had noticed it too and had tried to talk to me about it, but that's when I wound up punching him in the face instead. I felt about as bad as you could get. I didn't know what to do.

One of the best things about my little bookshop was it was across the way from the best little café in town. Whilst this did my waistline no favours, the combination of an award-winning bookshop next door to an award-winning café was a sensational pairing. Who doesn't like coffee, cake, and a good book? I attracted customers to them, and they attracted customers to me, a match made in heaven. I enjoyed the comings and goings of the customers and often watched them sit outside in the paved arcade, laughing and interacting, envious of their normality.

Phil and Anne had just had morning tea at the café next door and were excited to check out the new bookstore in town. Well, to be honest, the wife was excited to check out the bookstore, but her husband, less so. Whilst Anne dove elbow deep into the shelves, Phil leant on the counter chatting to me. He introduced himself, extending his hand in greeting.

"Hi, I'm Phil," he said cheerily, "I hope you've been to the toilet because my missus is going to be here for a while", he grinned cheekily, both of us catching Anne's side eye and tut which made him grin even wider.

"All good," I replied. "We're open till five."

Jokingly he raised his finger to his lips, "Shh don't tell her that, we'll wind up sleeping here," he chuckled, catching Anne's side eye again.

Unperturbed, she continued to dig through the shelves. There was something strangely familiar about him I couldn't place. He was in his early 60s, not much taller than me, slight build but very wiry. Whilst we talked, he looked around a lot, scanning the room and checking the door constantly. Every few minutes he'd call out to his wife, making sure Anne was still in the shop. He was slightly flighty, not completely at ease. It was behaviour that was not altogether unusual to me, and strangely familiar.

Without warning, he turned and looked at me with deep curiosity. Then he said it: "So when were you diagnosed with PTSD?"

What?!

I had no idea what he was talking about. I was a primary school teacher come bookshop owner, living in the burbs, and a married mother of two. People like me don't get PTSD. I thought that's for war veterans, police, ambulance paramedics, firemen.

I felt instantly unwell, and I could feel the colour draining out of my face. What was it he saw in me? What made him say that? A mixture of embarrassment and fury surged through my body, and I had an overwhelming urge to throw him out, lock the door behind him and never open it again. I could see he immediately regretted the question; a shocked look came over his face, immediately giving way to confusion. He looked flustered and began apologising, "I'm so sorry," he whispered "I thought you knew."

"Knew what?" I snapped defensively.

Hearing the exchange, Anne appeared out of nowhere, apologising profusely. "Phil's a Vietnam Veteran," she said hurriedly. "We're in town to see a therapist who lives here. He specialises in treating Vietnam Veterans and PTSD."

It felt like all the air was sucked out of the room. My lungs burned as I struggled to breathe. Why my encounter with Phil felt so familiar began to flood my brain. The man in front of me could well have been my dad. Similar height, similar build, and similar behaviour. A full circle moment. My past was looking at me over the counter of my shop. Like a hamster on a wheel, I'd circled back to the beginning. I'd been running as fast as I could my whole life. A feeble attempt to outrun the past, but I discovered I hadn't been running in a line. I was running in a circle. It had taken me 40 years to get to the beginning again. I'd done everything to forget, to avoid the story, to deny anything happened, but I was paying for that denial with my mind, body, and spirit. Months had passed since the day I had punched my husband in the face, and still we hadn't talked about it.

Suddenly I realised the truth. You can try, but you can't outrun your past. I was stuck in the mud with no place to go and no way out of it until Phil and Anne walked into my shop. Phil reflected to me what I was but hadn't been able to see. A person living on a knife's edge where any slip could be a fatal one.

They became regulars in my shop. Every time they came to see their therapist, they'd call in to see me too. Phil was the first person who talked to me about trauma and what it does to a person. We had some profound conversations about the Vietnam War, and he gave me some insight as to what my dad might have gone through. He told me his biggest regret was not having help available sooner and how sad he was at losing years battling his demons. It wasn't long before I asked for the contact details of this therapist he raved about, and Phil handed me a card. It simply said Joeseph Riordan – Clinical Psychologist. I resolved to give him a call as I'd lost enough years already.

My sister Narelle and I, early 1970s

My mother, the late 1960s

19-year-old Dad at basic training for Vietnam

**Not a very happy Christmas with
Mum, Narelle and I, early 1970s**

Our family home in Townsville, 2018

Narelle, Jacqueline and I in Townsville, 1978

Mum, Narelle and I in Townsville, 1980

My husband Ricky, 2016

Phil 'Sparra' Newey and me, 2024

Joseph Riordan, Psychologist, 2024

The 500, one of the photoframes
in Townsville, RSL, 2018

ANZAC Memorial Park, Townsville
Photo credit: Scott Radford-Chisholm, 2020

Ricky and I, 2024

Peace at Last
Photo credit: Mel Watt Photography

**My teacher Mrs. Worthington and I,
second row from the bottom far left, 1974**

-Angel Cats and Horses-

Why the fuck did I listen to Phil? I thought as I dragged myself to the front door. Even though I knew it was time to seek professional help, going to see my psychologist Joe that first day was horrific. He'd come highly recommended; however, I was still sceptical about his ability to help me, and I was desperate for help. I can't recall what I was more worked up about- seeing a psychologist and what he might tell me about myself or if, like other failed attempts, he couldn't help me at all- what would I do then? The Star Wars geek in me started reciting that famous line by 'Princess Leia', "This is our most desperate hour. Help me, Obi-Wan Kenobi. You're my only hope." It's exactly how I felt. In hindsight, it was an unfair amount of pressure to place on my new therapist, and myself for that matter. Fortunately, he rose to the occasion. Thoughts of Star Wars didn't give me the usual comfort I needed, and I began working myself up until I could barely breathe, my memories heavily tainted by the experiences of seeking help that had gone before. Walking out to my car and getting in was close to one of the hardest things I've ever had to do. Every footstep reverberated through the earth as my feet dragged me forward; my mind was willing, but my body was vigorously protesting. I struggled to stay present fighting off panic. My heart raced, and I felt like I couldn't get enough air. But I couldn't turn back now. It wasn't an easy decision, but I knew deep down that if I didn't go today, then I'd never go any day, so I dug deep.

I began using some strategies I'd taught my students, some calming breaths, some positive self-talk, distracting myself by looking around, taking in the day and the sheer beauty of it – a crisp winter day in August, with a brilliant blue sky. Our wedding anniversary had been only two days before, and I'd promised my husband this. If I couldn't do it for me, I was sure as hell going to do it for him until I could do it for me.

Joe's office was off to the side of his house. I think it made it easier going to see him there than a clinical doctor's office. That would have been too much for me at that stage. It was like visiting someone rather than anything too intrusive. As I pulled into his driveway, a wave of relief washed over me. *I did it. I'm here*. While still very nervous, the sight of a friendly horse wandering up to meet me calmed me down immediately. Rather than sit on the veranda in the waiting seats, I thought I'd give the horse a scratch for a while. I have always loved horses and dreamt about having my own one day, but time and finances had made it easier to enjoy other peoples.

The horse let me pat her for a while, but once she realised I had nothing to offer her, she turned tail and pranced away across her dusty paddock. Though reluctant to take a seat, I convinced myself this was all part of the experience, so I made my way to the waiting area, the light fragrance of the friendly horse still lingering around me. I focused on it, taking comfort in the scent as I moved forwards up the three steps towards the veranda above. Before I reached the seats, a sliding door on the side of the house opened, catching me by surprise; before I got the chance to panic, Joe had collected me from the doorstep and delivered me safely to his office. To this day, I have absolutely no recollection of what happened between the door opening and sitting down inside. Later in my therapy, I'd learn about disassociation, and I'd finally be able to account for my lost memories over time, but for this day just getting in the door was an accomplishment and one I'm proud of.

Once settled, I loved Joe's office. It wasn't like any I'd ever been in before. Apart from the obvious difference of it being in a house it felt more like visiting an old friend in their front sitting room rather than a formal doctor's office. The room was decorated with children's drawings, in particular an 'Angel Cat' which had been drawn by Joe's granddaughter. It hung proudly on the wall and sat just over his shoulder as you looked at him. Its cheery innocence appealed to my inner little girl, and something about it made me feel safe and happy. That little angel cat grounded me more times than I can say, and when Joe eventually built a new office when he expanded the business to include his daughter, that little angel cat came with him, looking lovingly down on every session we spent together. To this day, I can still see it in my mind's eye and with it, that sense of safety and comfort I had in that room will return to me. Joe was well travelled and had little artifacts from here and there, which helped make small talk and bring me into the room. A beautiful Ganesha stood on the top shelf of the display cabinet, rather fitting that the remover of obstacles would also come on this journey with me. Before long, I was sipping on a cup of tea and talking about why I had sought him out whilst he leaned over and dropped lavender oil on a banksia nut sitting on a side table.

From that first session, it struck me that no one had ever listened to me like Joe did. I realise now that other therapists had gone wrong because they talked at me. They wanted to tell me what was 'wrong' with me and try to 'fix' me after barely knowing me for five minutes. It was a very long time before Joe offered any type of 'diagnosis' per se and that was only after I asked him what he thought was going on with me. Looking back on the first few months of therapy I don't know how Joe did it. He literally sat there listening to me for an hour straight every fortnight, barely getting a word in, holding space with such care and compassion that all sorts of truths started coming out of my mouth. Stories I'd told no one – not even my husband – were left hanging in the air of Joe's home office, whilst the smell of coffee and home cooking filtered down the hallway. All the sadness, the fear, the grief, the abuse left out in the open for someone else to see and he believed me. I can't tell you the abject relief I felt unburdening myself from the weight of fear and secrecy to a person who listened. I don't have and never will have the words to thank him for the space he gave me to just speak every word I'd never been allowed to for 40 years.

Over time we discussed the difficulties I'd faced in my childhood. How unwell my mother had been through her life and how her erratic and unpredictable behaviour had me walking on eggshells. I spoke of my dad and how scared he'd made me feel, how he'd made my sister eat the food that she'd thrown up on her plate and how he'd made me watch as he slapped her poor tiny leg, 10 times or more, because she'd left cups in her room. How I'd been powerless to stop him again and again. I grieved with him about the lost childhood I'd never reclaim, how I'd given it up looking after my sisters and my mother, and how often I stayed up with her just to keep her alive. We talked about the pride I had in being the first person in my family to finish school and go to university and how truly hard it was to break that cycle. How I'd lived in a car at university after Mum got us evicted from housing commission because she gambled away the rent. I talked about how breaking that cycle created so much tension between my mother and I she tried her very best to sabotage my education, fearing she'd lose me, ultimately ruining my first attempt at university and costing me a $20,000 HECS debt with my second. We talked about being so scared at school that I carried half a brick in my bag so I could keep bullies at bay and how sometimes that didn't work, and I'd get beaten up for being smart, or having red hair or just existing. My heart ached with shame as I confessed about the time I stole food from the local convenience store because I couldn't stand my little sisters going to bed hungry another night in a row and I flamed in anger over the time I was given a detention at school for not watching the handing down of the budget for homework as no one would believe I didn't have a TV. It was in the pawnshop, but I was too ashamed to tell the teacher and took the punishment instead. Years later, when Facebook became a thing and someone from school found me, the first thing they asked was, "Weren't you the girl who didn't have a TV?"

I cried, when I finally let myself over every time I looked out into the crowd at an awards ceremony, and no one was there for me. I felt the pang of rejection recalling ringing every pub in Campbelltown on my 18th birthday trying to find my mum but couldn't. By the end, I don't think there was much Joe didn't know about me. For once I didn't feel ashamed. It felt good to finally let someone through the wall and we began taking it down together, brick by brick.

Whilst it had felt amazing to get a lot of things off my chest, I was still experiencing a lot of the problems that had taken me to therapy. Sometimes I was so agoraphobic I wouldn't leave the house for weeks on end. I got paranoid and had anxiety attacks thinking if I had a meltdown in public someone might film me and share it on social media. I'd imagine I'd change from the girl without a TV to the crazy lady at Coles. My anxiety was so high I could barely sleep for more than a few hours at a time, and I was so exhausted I could easily go for a week or so without taking a shower. You so rarely hear of the health impacts that living with mental health issues has on people and I hadn't really considered how my mental health was impacting my physical health. The constant levels of high stress and fatigue were taking its toll on me. I had been getting my mental health in order, but it wasn't translating to my body. Poor eating or not eating at all caused issues with my blood sugar, I had high cholesterol, I was overweight, I had chronic gum disease and at risk of losing my teeth because I was terrified of the dentist and found it hard to attend to my own personal hygiene. I hadn't had a pap smear in about a decade or walked into a doctor's surgery for around four years. I paid full price for my psychology appointments to avoid dealing with the anxiety inducing medical system. Sadly, women can reduce their life expectancy by 9-17 years when they have severe mental health issues and that's what I was facing. With genuine concerns for my physical health, I decided I had to take my therapy with Joe into new territory which involved facing my demons, reconnecting to my body, and learning to love myself exactly as I am.

-A Diagnosis and a Disappointment-

"**I**'m worried I might be a psychopath."

Across the room two greying eyebrows gently rose, a quizzical look spreading across Joe's face.

"Why's that, Christina?"

"Well…" I paused, trying to find the right words. "Something is wrong with me… What else could it be?"

By this time, I was three years into my therapy and was feeling increasingly confused by my lack of emotion. In the past 12 weeks, I'd lost my grandparents and whilst everyone else around me was falling apart, I was taking care of everything. I had executed their wills with mechanical precision and made sure their funerals were arranged. And yet, as much as I loved them, I was finding it very hard to feel much at all, and it bothered me a lot.

Joe smiled at me, looking more amused than anything else. I wasn't sure if the thought of me being a psychopath was laughable or he found my attempts at armchair psychology amusing, but to my relief he replied with as straight a face as he could muster, "No Christina, I don't believe you are a psychopath."

Even though I didn't want to be a psychopath, I began rattling off all the reasons I thought I was to a man with over 30 years' experience as a psychologist and a published expert on trauma. Of particular concern to me was the constant feeling of being numb. I didn't seem to have any discernible feelings or emotions in everyday life, and this was the first time I'd properly noticed. After patiently listening to my rambling Joe finally said, "Do you really want to know what I think is going on for you, or do you want to keep talking yourself into being a psychopath?"

That was a great question.

Well, did I?

It felt like a lot of time passed before I finally answered, "Well, I suppose so. I came here to figure this out."

"Yes, you did," Joe replied with his signature brand of calm – a splash of wisdom thrown in for good measure.

He ran his hand over the top of his balding head and said in a very matter of fact kind of way, "Christina. For most of your life, you haven't felt safe. As a child, you didn't have your basic needs met. You were not cared for in the way children should be. You were exposed to violence and poverty, and you had to grow up quicker than you should have. Taking all that into consideration, I believe you have CPTSD – Complex Post Traumatic Stress Disorder.”

Well, what do you know… Phil was bloody right.

I knew nothing about PTSD except that it was something that affected soldiers and first responders, so to hear that diagnosis to begin with was confusing. As Joe took me through the symptoms it became more and more obvious to me he was right. My next question had a more serious tone to it, and I could tell by the look on Joe’s face he had likely guessed what it was.

“Can it be cured?”

The words hung tightly in the air, hope holding them aloft. But when I investigated Joe’s face, I could tell the answer was going to be no. To say I was angry about that is an understatement. Seriously what was the damn point of three years of therapy if I couldn’t be cured? As a society we’ve been so entrained to think that everything can be fixed or cured, doctors can perform all sorts of miracles all the time; they just couldn’t do it for me. My heart sank and felt like it broke into a million pieces. Hot tears filled my eyes, and rage was building in my body. Before I totally went ballistic, Joe quickly explained that my childhood trauma had changed my brain physiology and whilst that couldn’t be changed back, there had been lots of new and exciting advancements in the treatment of trauma. He began explaining that he had been researching Somatic Therapy for quite some time and was very interested in the research of Dr. Peter Levine. Joe explained that he’d begun writing his own paper about trauma and had trained with Dr.

Levine in Somatic Experiencing, as well as EDMR and Tremor Release Exercises. Whilst Joe couldn't offer me the 'cure' I had so desperately hoped for, he did offer a treatment that could significantly calm my dysregulated nervous system if I wanted to try it.

"Okay… How do we start?" I asked.

On that day, I said yes to the next part of my journey; I literally had nothing to lose.

-Somatic Experiencing-

I'm not going to lie. When I first started somatic experiencing, it was hard work. I hated it, and it did not go well.

At first, it felt like it highlighted just how messed up I was, and that made me feel worse than I already did. The simple task of just sitting in a chair and paying attention to my body sensations was so foreign to me it scared me. I'd spent so much time consumed by surviving I'd never sat quietly with myself. The only time I'd ever paid attention to how my body felt was if I was checking for injury or to make sure I was still alive so trying to notice the other ways my body felt was a real challenge. My constant hypervigilance made it difficult to sit with my eyes closed, even in Joe's office, where I felt safe and had complete trust in him. I'd keep interrupting the process by talking and trying to explain things. I'd want to attach a story to every feeling; wanting to know why I was feeling something seemed to be more important to me than simply feeling it. I was trying to think my way through like I always had rather than feel my way through like I needed to, and I could not for the life of me, get my head around the difference. I'd been disconnected from my body for so long I was genuinely fearing I'd never reconnect. If I felt something, then what might happen???

I'd almost get there, but I'd constantly cycle back to trying to talk my way out of discomfort, a futile exercise that I knew didn't work, but it didn't stop me trying. I'd show up for sessions that I knew were scheduled for somatic work, but I'd waste the whole time talking about lots of irrelevant things to avoid the processes. Joe knew he'd have to change tactics.

"Next session, come in clothes you'd work out in," Joe said, completely out of the blue.

He graciously hadn't commented about my avoidance of doing the somatic work I had whole heartedly said I wanted to do. He had approached this part of my therapy with the same patience and compassion our talk sessions had. If I was frustrating him, I never knew it, but I was sure as heck frustrating the life out of myself. *How hard can it be to just sit in a chair and feel things?* I thought. I have always been my own worst critic and the severe talks I'd give myself after every 'failed' session just added to the anxiety I was feeling.

I'd taken my physical health more seriously and had engaged with a personal trainer, so Joe knew I had workout clothes and a good tolerance for exercise. He discussed the idea of taking a break from the somatic work of interoception, just trying to get my executive brain to notice what was going on in my nervous system and try another type of body work called Tremor Release Exercises (TRE). He promised he wouldn't ask me to feel anything at all, just lay down, lift my pelvis off the ground and set off shaking in my body. Well, it's a little more complicated than that, but it gives you the general picture of what he was asking me to do. Joe, appealing to my scientific curiosity and love of animals, went on to explain that Peter Levine had noticed that prey animals escaping a predator inevitably trembled and shook for some time after the traumatic event. Once their tremors subsided, the prey animal would run off as if nothing had happened. As a girl I had noticed that too. I had once taken a baby rat from a cat's mouth and the poor thing sat for a half hour shaking in my hands. It suddenly stopped and ran off before I had the chance to notice. Joe had piqued my curiosity. He explained the tremoring uses up all the stress hormones the body naturally produces during times of distress, so inducing tremoring gave the body a chance to process the trauma locked deep within my body. This sounded easy and interesting, so I gave it a go.

The first tremoring experience was excellent. My backside was barely in the air before my body began tremoring. It was only small at first, starting in my quads and moving into my stomach. The tremor built with such momentum that in no time at all my whole body was involved. I lay there shaking and shivering on the floor of Joe's home gym without a single care in the world. I felt like something reconnected in my body. I felt whole and emotionally switched on and alive. Peter Levine calls this the natural goodness of living, the felt sense, and that is exactly the best way to describe it. It was almost euphoric. After a few minutes or so, it subsided, and I felt extremely relaxed and calm and could have easily gone off to sleep. Shaking off, as I now call it, became part of my nighttime routine and helped me sleep a lot better than I ever had. I found my body would just spontaneously shake as I lay down in bed and I'd let it, not trying to find a story or a reason. With my confidence restored, Joe talked about Somatic

Experiencing again, and this time I was a lot more successful. He explained that whilst the TRE was helpful in relieving traumatic tension in my body, the Somatic Experiencing would work more on my brain and nervous system. The idea was to teach my body and brain to work together not against each other, so I could finally feel safe.

Ultimately, I began to enjoy Somatic Experiencing and would always feel so much lighter after it. Sometimes I'd twitch and tremble during it, sometimes I'd cry, sometimes I'd burn hot and sometimes I'd be so cold I'd need a blanket, sometimes I'd feel like stretching my whole body out as far as it could go and sometimes I'd feel like running around. When I was very comfortable with the process Joe began adding extra elements to it. If he noticed me making a fist, he would give me something to punch into, in a slow exaggerated way allowing my body to complete a survival action it had always wanted to do. He noticed me pushing away with my feet so would bring the coffee table over and hold it in place so I could push as hard as I could against it to let my legs finish the pushing action started somewhere a long time ago, but never finished. Every movement, every word, every feeling and every emotion that had never been safe to express had been trapped in my body for decades and when given the chance had burst free with vigour. Sometimes Joe's face morphed into my dad's as he held a cushion in front of me, allowing me the chance to punch and hit in a slow and deliberate motion. His firm hand behind the cushion providing resistance to push into. I got to say all I wanted to but never had. Joe always skilfully keeping me from going too far so I wouldn't dissociate. I could literally feel the shifting in my brain as it pendulated between trauma and safety, teaching me that not every uncomfortable feeling I had was going to result in me being hurt or dying. I stopped trying to figure out the 'why' of everything and just allowed my body the space it needed to heal from all the wrongs it had been through. I became so comfortable with Somatic Experiencing I even did it once hanging onto a ladder on the side of a boat in Vanuatu.

After many sessions, I began to feel like I inhabited my body again and that I had some control over my actions and reactions. My body had started out as a driverless bus, reacting violently to every pothole, horn blast or traffic jam, but when my mind reconnected to my body, I decided how the bus was going to be driven, which roads to take, how to avoid potholes and if I hit one, I handled it a whole lot better. I stopped being at the mercy of my survival lizard brain. Whilst it had served me well and I was alive because of it, it didn't need to be in operation 24/7. Somatic work gave me a big toolbox to use when the going got tough. My brain had shut down my feelings long ago to protect me, but I didn't need it to do that anymore. The problem with shutting out negative feelings is you wind up shutting out all your feelings, and it becomes harder and harder to reach them again and I was going to need access to all the feelings I could if I was going to handle what was ahead of me.

-Anni Horribilis-

Some people say, *What doesn't kill you makes you stronger.* I say those people can stick that saying where the sun doesn't shine. I didn't want to be strong; I wanted to be happy. The years between 2013 and 2020 were impossibly difficult ones for me. Not only was I dedicated to getting healthy and addressing all the issues that came from a lifetime of abuse; I also had to deal with a revolving door of family illnesses and funerals. I'd lose seven loved ones in seven years, including my mum and my dad. This enforced timeline expediated my date with destiny.

Joe had been talking to me for some time about the concept of Dyadic Completion. In lay terms I had to integrate my childhood memories of violence, neglect, and manipulation into adult ones of survival, love and safety. I needed to understand that my parents couldn't hurt me anymore, and that they were damaged adults who were overwhelmed by their own mental health issues that had brought violence and dysfunction into our family. Whilst I could cognitively understand that as an adult, I was safe, no matter how much work I was putting into my healing, it took little to drag me back to those memories of times when I wasn't. My relationships with my parents, particularly my dad, were as we left them when I was a child, and literally incomplete. My relationship between my parents and me was still in trauma. We had never had the chance to heal the terrible rupture that had occurred between us in my childhood. My core memories were those of a child and those memories were full of neglect and violence. I needed my adult self to see I was safe now and the best way to do that was working things through with my parents. I knew, through my sister, that Dad was in poor health and realised I didn't have long to meet with him, but what I didn't expect was that Mum would go first.

It was July 2017 and just seven months after we'd lost our wonderful brother-in-law Andy in a truck crash at work. He was only 35. I've done nothing harder in my life than having to collect his ashes and deliver them to my baby sister as she lay weeping on her lounge room floor. Our family was in turmoil, reeling from the loss of a young man who had his whole life ahead of him. In part, it was the loss of Andy that made me decide what I had to do to get my life back. He made me think about how precious life is and how I didn't want to waste another minute of it being held hostage by ghosts from my past. The time had come to deal with the remaining dyadic trauma between me and my parents.

When Joe first explained the idea of Dyadic Completion with me, I was absolutely against it. I'd have to get myself back to Townsville and wander through the haunted corridors of my childhood. That was a hard no. However, when Andy died, it changed everything for me. He and my sister had this big, beautiful life planned, travelling, building a home together and lots of love, and it was all gone just like that. I felt an overwhelming sadness about all the things I'd already missed out on because of fear, and I didn't want that anymore. I'd began having more serious conversations with Joe about going to see Dad in Townsville when I got the news.

One afternoon, Mum called to tell me she'd been admitted to hospital as she wasn't well and would like to see me. Her tone lacked its usual dramatic flair and that worried me. She insisted we talk in person. "This isn't something I want to tell you over the phone," she said.

She had been diagnosed with the same cancer that had taken my grandmother in only 12 weeks, so we knew the news was dire and she wouldn't have long with us. Somatic work had been a game changer in helping me connect to my body. However, being body aware had only helped me manage my symptoms of PTSD and I wanted healing that would go deeper than that. Time was now running out to heal myself when it came to my mother and the trauma we shared.

I had long let go of the expectations I had around what a mother was meant to be. It was easier that way. It released the pressure on her and lowered the disappointment for me. I'd come to think of her as my irresponsible older sister. We'd had so many conversations about her smoking and drinking and how it would impact her health, and she'd just laugh and say, "Christina you worry too much. I'm here for a good time, not a long time."

She was right. Mum only had weeks left on earth and time was running out for both of us. I really didn't know how I was going to do it. I just knew I had to, but her terminal diagnosis made me feel like a horrible daughter, a selfish person who was only thinking about me. This was exactly how she had trained me to see myself. It had kept me on her lead like a pet dog for way too long, and it was time to put it to an end.

-Angel Mother-

It had been several weeks since we had been told Mum would not have long to live. She was back in hospital and had sent me a message that she wanted to see me right away. The hour-long drive felt like forever. Wondering what was so urgent that she had to see me so quickly, had me pumping with anxiety. A thousand scenarios played in my head, but I was hopelessly unprepared for what she said.

Truth be told, I had been avoiding her the best I could but something about her message made me feel like this was a conversation I wasn't going to be able to avoid. My mother was dying, and I didn't know how to feel about it. With her lifestyle, I knew this was inevitable, but now it was here, I didn't seem that worried about it. I began questioning what sort of person I was. Who doesn't care that their mother is dying? Even terminally ill mum was still messing with my head. As I walked closer to her hospital room, I began feeling sick. All those times I'd been summoned and hurt started flooding my memories. Slippers thrown and missed; *bring it back to me Christina*, and wack. *Come to the kitchen Christina;* plates thrown and wack. *Here, come meet my friends Christina;* don't embarrass me and wack. What could she possibly want from me? Did I even want to know? She was going to die and get away, but I would be left with this conversation for the rest of my life, so I was going to have to tread carefully. The little girl in me was urging me to leave, but the woman I'd become needed this.

I turned the final corner that led to her room. She was in a public hospital in Brisbane, and I found her still in her shared ward of four, sleeping on her bed. She had tried to get herself moved to a private room but apparently to no avail. I sat gently on the chair beside her. A stiff hospital chair designed to keep the visit short and restless. Her chest was heavy and her breath raspy and my heart skipped a beat with the realisation she was really sick. This wasn't one of her dramas she had made up for attention. Looking at her laying there, you could see the cancer was starting to consume her. Her complexion was grey and dry and her once beautiful face that had made so many men do crazy things, was sunken in and hollow. Her hair now brittle and grey gently fell across her face and I felt a pang of sadness for the times I'd sat behind her brushing her long, thick red locks whilst she watched Sale of the Century drinking many glasses of Bacardi. This rare happy memory brought a temporary smile to my face and released some of the tension. I sat there staring at her, wishing she could have been the mother I needed her to be. Now there was no more time left. In that moment I decided to accept that she was who she was once and for all.

I sat quietly watching her sleep. My awareness of our often-reversed roles washed over me. I'd frequently been the parent in our relationship, and I would be to the last. Even at her worst I had never left her side and I began to wonder what final things were going to be asked of me. Slowly Mum stirred, and I could feel my apprehension rise. She spotted me almost immediately smiling broadly, "Hi kiddo, I knew you'd come. You're always there when I open my eyes."

I really didn't like when she called me that. It meant she was buttering me up for something, so I just had to hold my breath and wait to see what it was going to be.

"We've had a good life together you and I, haven't we?" she said very quietly, almost as if she was trying to convince herself and ask me at the same time.

How to answer.

Before my answer came, she looked straight at me. Her faded blue eyes met mine and I could feel her stare reaching into my heart and soul.

"I was a good mother, wasn't I?" she asked.

This is what she had called me all the way to Brisbane for?

I can't begin to imagine what goes through a person's mind when they have been told they don't have long to live, but it was clear to me in that moment, Mum had been reflecting a lot and it sounded like she had some regrets. What a position to put me in. After all I had gone through with her, she had waited until she was on her death bed to ask if she was a good mother; now she asks. I desperately wanted to yell at the top of my lungs, "No Mum, you were a terrible mother, you were the worst, you ignored me, you hurt me, you starved me, you stole my childhood from me, you did nothing to encourage me, you made me feel like I was a worthless human being who had no right to be here!" but I couldn't utter a word. Saying anything like that to a dying woman just would not do and she knew it. It was another one of her gotcha moments where you have to say exactly the right thing or you are the arsehole, and there's no bigger one than the arsehole who tells their mother she sucked on her deathbed. I did not want to play this game anymore. I could not sit here and tell my mother how great she had been. I could not disrespect that little girl who had never felt wanted, who never had a birthday party, who grew up sooner than she ought to; the little girl who never felt safe, who never looked out from a concert or assembly stage and saw her mother there. I could not disrespect myself and tell this woman, regardless of her illness, that she had been a good mother to me. I just couldn't. But I wouldn't destroy a sick woman and send her to her grave humiliated and feeling unloved. Because I did love her. She had been through enough in her life and I would not treat her how she had treated me.

As we sat looking at each other in silence I felt a calm come over me. I could feel my sense of self grow as I began to carefully consider the words I would choose that could honour me and my experiences without landing a fatal blow on my mother's heart.

Mum's expression changed from hopeful to worried as I contemplated those words and when I began to speak, for once she did not interrupt.

I reached out to my mother and held her hand and said with loving care, "Mum. What you need to appreciate is that you and I have very different memories of our life together. Sometimes we had a lot of fun together and I'm sure you tried your best to be a good mother."

Tears started to fall down her face, but she did not disagree.

I went on respectfully, "What you need to remember is that for a good part of my life with you, you struggled with addiction and I'm glad for you that you don't have some of the memories that I do. These addictions made it so that you were not always your best self and sometimes that made life very hard for my sisters and me. For the sake of what time we have left together, I don't really think questions like that at this stage are going to be helpful to either of us."

I took a huge deep breath, and a weight lifted from my shoulders. I felt strong and powerful. It was the first time I had properly felt like an adult in my mother's presence. I had spoken my truth and my mother respected it. For the first time in my life, I felt like her daughter and not her mother. Still holding her hands in mine, I stood up and kissed her on the head. She looked up at me, her tear-stained face formed into a small smile.

"I've always loved you, you know" she said, I could feel the sincerity in her voice.

But holding tightly to my position, I gently replied, "I know that Mum, even if it wasn't always obvious."

The truth between us was then known, but unspoken.

Suddenly her mood changed, and she became very serious and resolute, "Do you think I'll go to hell?" she whispered, trying to make sure no one else could hear her.

"No Mum, you haven't done anything bad enough for that," I replied.

She slumped back in her bed with a sigh of relief and asked, "Do you think I'll be an angel?"

The idea of my mum being an angel greatly appealed to me and out of nowhere I said to her, "Yes Mum, I think you will be an angel. You'll be our angel mother, and you'll get to do all the things for us I know you wanted to, but just couldn't in this lifetime. You'll be able to look over us and keep us safe. You are going to be the best angel mother there ever was."

She smiled at me and said, "I'll look forward to that."

I let go of her hands and scooped her into my arms and hugged her deeply. "So will I Mum," I said, tears rolling down my face and into her hair.

The idea of finally having her care for me the way I needed her too even if it was in angelic form, gave me a sense of peace. My love for her burst through my heart and I finally felt something.

That would be the final conversation I ever got to have with my mother.

A few days later her health catastrophically failed, and she barely hung on long enough for everyone to get there and say goodbye. Mum had been there for my first breath, and I was there for her last. I held her hand until the end, just like I promised.

That night I went home and wrote myself a letter from my mother. I wrote everything that I always wished she had said to me. Maybe she would have if she had been able. I wept until there were no more tears and when I finally could, I read her letter to myself aloud. I had never once been validated by my mother. My very existence had been a mistake and ruined her life according to her, so hearing what I'd imagined my mother would have said if she could have profoundly healed my heart.

I can't imagine how hard her life was, having been that unwell and never getting to live the life she dreamed of. It was hard to stay angry and disappointed when I was sitting in compassion and love for a fellow mother who never got on top of her issues. I took mum's letter down to my backyard and burned it. I sent the words in smoke to the heavens so my angel mother could be reunited with them, as I'm certain it was she who guided my hand that night. As the letter burned, I whispered, "I love you Mum, I know you did the best you could with what you had," and then the letter was gone and my pain along with it.

Healing our shared trauma left me free to love my angel mother without fear, resentment, pain, powerlessness, or fear of abandonment.

-Castle Hill, Mt. Stuart, and the Sugar Shaker-

After the passing of my mother, my thoughts returned to the idea of addressing issues with my dad. When Joe first raised the idea of returning to Townsville, initially it had been a solid no. Whilst the thought of returning to Townsville had filled me with dread, I realised there was a lot more to it than that. After my parents' separation, my mother had commanded complete loyalty to her, and I'd given it. Not only did I not want to return to Townsville; I didn't want to betray her. Reaching out to my dad would have been seen as the ultimate act of betrayal and the ramifications I'd likely get for it contributed to my feelings of reluctance to go. With the death of my mother, that obstacle had been removed, so I explored the idea of Dyadic Completion with more rigour.

At this point I would like to convey the amount of work and preparation that went into venturing up to Townsville. This is not something I did lightly, and I don't recommend confronting an abuser from your past without giving it due consideration and having lots of planning and support. When I made the decision to go back to Townsville, I had been working on myself with my very experienced psychologist Joe for many years and have an incredibly supportive husband whom I trust with my life. Even with those two compelling factors in place, it was still a massive enterprise to consider. It isn't my intention to suggest that this course of action is appropriate for everyone. I just wish to express this is something I wanted to do, to support my next level of healing.

With all my safety plans in place and Joe on speed dial, the day had arrived. I was going back to Townsville.

It was October 2018 and the flight to see my dad in Townsville was the longest flight of my life. Everything about it was painful. The seatbelt across my lap felt constricted and suffocating. The sense of being immobilised again set off every safety trigger in me. There wasn't anywhere in my body that felt safe or calm. Every inch of my skin thrummed with adrenalin, run little one run, it whispered in my ears, but again there was nowhere to run too. My legs, too short to reach the floor of the plane dangled childlike in the air. My feet began paddling playing out what my body wanted to do – run. I was struggling to stay present, flicking between child and adult with every blink of my eye.

Joe and I had talked at length about what my body might do during this journey and what strategies I could engage to ease it, but now I was in the throes of it, I feared I wouldn't use them. A news reel started playing in my head showing me the outcome if I did not get it together. And tonight, on Channel Nine News, a flight to Townsville was forced to land when a woman on board caused a disturbance. I didn't want that to be the end of my story.

I knew going to Townsville would be confronting, but how confronting was just revealing itself. Just after take-off, nausea began rising in my body. I broke out into a heavy sweat and the seat was becoming saturated. I could feel the rivulets of sweat pouring down my back and pooling in my butt cheeks. I began shaking in my seat. A small tremor at first growing and growing until my whole body became a jiggling mass of flesh. I looked around the plane. Connecting to the here and now would allow me to stay present and grounded, helping fight off the dissociation which was struggling for control. I counted the windows and listened to the low murmur of the passengers around me. I could feel the support of the chair beneath me and the cool puff of air conditioning blowing down from overhead. Breathe. The angel cat appeared out of the mist and into my mind's eye. I was winning this battle. As I slowed down my breathing, I felt my husband's loving hand alongside my leg – not on me but next to me, a reassuring touch from someone I loved brought me fully back into my body. I didn't get that close to losing it again.

To stay grounded and connected to my body I continued to look around. As I did it struck me how different this plane journey was compared to the last time I'd flown to Townsville, nearly nine-years-old sitting alongside my heavily pregnant mother and seven-year-old sister. Apart from wings and seats nearly all of it was different. No one was smoking, people were dressed like they were going to the pub, the flight attendants didn't look like models and the cabin was so quiet, no low-level drone of engines carrying us on our way. This time my husband sat by me, our love, and his love for me had made so much possible. To be truly loved exactly as I am is a gift I can't explain; mere words could not do it justice. To love someone back the same way fills me with peace and inner strength. It was this peace and inner strength I needed now. I was doing this for him as much as I was for me. By healing this wound with my dad, I hoped I could become the person I wanted to be. I still had so much of my life ahead of me and I was choosing happiness. Last time I came here, I was just a little girl. This time, I was a woman. Only months away from turning 50, I was using this milestone birthday as a life reset button. I wasn't going to get this chance again so losing it in the plane wasn't an option. Trying to calm myself I started thinking of things that made me feel good or happy. Ricky noticed me calming down and then smiling. "You good?" he asked carefully.

"I am", I said calmly. "I'm just thinking about how much I love you, how much I love our kids and how great it's going to be to put this part of my life to bed."

He took my hand, his radiant warmth instantly spread through my body. I began chanting in my head, *Peace and strength Christina, peace and strength.* It was my mantra until we landed.

As Mt. Stuart came into sight, I knew we weren't far from landing. I had grown up looking at the mountain from my bedroom window. It had been the silent witness to every atrocity that had unfolded in our household. Now it would be a witness to my return. Now Mt. Stuart would see a woman claim her sovereignty and take her life back. I'd returned home to pick up my little girl whom I'd left alone, holding onto a story too big for her to handle.

-A Woman's Return-

When I reached out to Dad to let him know Ricky and I were coming to Townsville for a week to make sure he'd be there, I hadn't told him much about why. I wasn't sure how it was going to pan out or if I'd even have the courage to face him so I decided to go with the story that I hadn't been to Townsville since I was a little girl and would love to see how it was now. I wanted to show Ricky the house I'd grown up in and my old school and perhaps pop over to Magnetic Island. Ricky had never been to Townsville before, so half of the story was true. I had told him where I was staying, but little else. I had refused an offer of borrowing his car or staying anywhere he had arranged; I didn't want to be obligated to him. My experience with Mum was the few things she did do for me had come with strings attached and that wasn't a price I was willing to pay. I was sovereign. I'd pay my own way.

As we disembarked the plane, I had to walk across the tarmac again, retracing the steps I took in January 1978. It was a surreal experience walking between two worlds, both existing at the same time, eight-year-old me and 49-year-old me occupying the same space at the same time. I glanced to my right and a swear I could see a little red-haired girl in shiny black shoes walking alongside me. I reached out my hand to her and said to myself, *We've got this,* as I followed my husband to the terminal.

The inside of Townsville airport was completely different from how I had remembered it. Totally refurbished and set up to greet the growing tourism industry, it had a happy welcoming feeling, and I felt at ease. I had arrived in Townsville. Step one of the journey. Barring my small hiccup on the plane, I was happy with how I was travelling, and began looking forward to exploring my old childhood stomping ground with my husband at my side. We just had to collect our bags, pick up the hire car and check into the hotel, which was on The Strand overlooking Magnetic Island a short drive from the airport. Literally everything in Townsville is a short drive from the airport. As I reached the top of the escalator, I looked down and there was my dad standing there waiting for me. I hadn't expected him to be there and hadn't invited him. He had just shown up. I wasn't ready yet! I thought I'd have a day to settle in. I thought I'd have more time. *You've had 41 years Christina,* my internal voice said, *How much longer do you need?*

I had less than a minute on the escalator to decide what to do. *Well played, Dad,* was the first thought that came to mind. He had met me in a public place, less chance of a scene, and I certainly couldn't attack him with so many witnesses and camera's around. *That's it,* I thought, *No more true crime documentaries for you.* What hadn't occurred to me in all this planning was how my dad was going to feel about seeing me. My sisters had already had it out with Dad and I'm sure they would have told him how strong and independent I had become. Of the three sisters, I was the one you did not want to mess with. How did he know I wasn't going to get off the plane, tell him what I thought of him, turn around and fly back home? He didn't; yet had shown up anyway. I realised I had the upper hand; I was in no danger and looking at the man standing before me confirmed that realisation. An old frail man barely standing unassisted had wobbled his way to the bottom of the escalator. I could see each step was causing insurmountable pain, but still he walked. Gone was his straight back and powerful arms that had struck so many painful blows. He was slouched over now, and his arms hung loosely at his sides. The image of my dad in his 30s, the monster that I always saw when I closed my eyes, gave way to this old grey-haired man. The man in front of me could easily be pushed over and run away from. His face was now fully bearded and his hair well below the collar, a no no in his army years. As I descended the escalator, he lifted his chin and braced himself, ready to receive whatever it was I was bringing him in Townsville. As I edged closer, his eyes met mine, slight fear behind them. I'd left a girl but returned a woman and he could see that. The noises of the airport faded away as the escalator delivered me unceremoniously to his feet. He and I became the only two people left in the world, connected through trauma and pain, both of us wearing it on our faces and in our bodies. Both of us now presented with the opportunity to dig through our wardrobes of skeletons and give them a decent burial. In that moment this stopped being about me and became about both of us. Two souls united by trauma. I could see he was desperate to connect with me, but the foyer of Townsville airport was not the time or place for that, and I wasn't ready. I'd be doing this on my terms or not at all. As I stepped toward him, he didn't move or flinch. He dropped his chin and looked at his feet like a child who had just been caught doing something they shouldn't. I could sense the heaviness of the weight he was carrying, and a pang of sadness gripped my heart. I couldn't bring myself to embrace him, instead offering a small wave in greeting. "Hi Dad, I didn't expect to see you here," I said trying to use a bright indifferent voice.

"Ah well there's not that many flights a day into Townsville from Brisbane, so I thought I'd take my chances that you'd be on this one," he said, a definite tone of relief in his voice.

Ricky stood next to me, but slightly behind me, close enough to step in if things went pear shaped but far enough away to give us the space we needed. As an awkward silence started to grow between us, Ricky, being the gentleman he is, broke the ice by warmly shaking my dad's hand, introducing himself and suggesting we all move towards the baggage collection.

"That might be a bit far for these old legs," Dad said quietly, "How about I wait here until you come back? I'll give you a lift to the hotel."

"No need," I chirped, "We've organised a hire car. We didn't want to disrupt you getting about town."

"Oh", he replied, his eyes cast downward. "Well, I might start heading out to my car then, I'll meet you at the hotel," he said eager to prolong his time with me.

Whilst organising the trip, I had mentioned in passing where we would stay when Dad had offered to arrange accommodation for us. It hadn't occurred to me he'd want to go there. Panic started swirling in my stomach and I became rooted in place. Speech evaded me, and I didn't know what to do. A freeze response was making itself felt in my body and my husband recognised the signs; stepping forward he said, "That's not necessary Jim, I'll give you a ring when we've settled and maybe we can meet later for dinner?"

Not taking the hint, Dad soldiered on, "Na, mate it's no problem. What type of host would I be if I didn't help you settle in?" and he hobbled away to his car.

Powerless to stop him, I just stood there, like a marble statue in a museum, feeling cold, with nothing to say. Once Dad was out of sight, Ricky hugged me. "You've got this," he whispered in my ear. *You're damn right*, I thought.

The journey to our hotel took about 20 minutes. Apart from Castle Hill, Mount Stuart, and the Sugar Shaker Hotel, I recognised no other landmarks. It was like a whole other city that I hadn't seen before. As we drove closer to the coast, Magnetic Island came into sight. I was flooded with childhood memories of the one time I went there. My grandmother driving around in a mini-moke, her beautiful smile and shiny red hair, her jolly laughter and her bright blue eyes were clear in my mind, just like it was yesterday. A pang of missing her clutched my heart. What I'd do for one more hug. Pushing that aside, I reminded myself of what I'd come here for. Whilst reminiscing was nice, there'd have to be time for that later.

As the hotel came into sight, I spotted a crowd of people gathered on the footpath. They were tending to an old man who was heavily bleeding. He looked like he'd had a fall. As we came closer, I realised in horror the old man was my dad. The image of the monster who had haunted my dreams and waking hours vanished and, in its place, sat a frail old man barely able to hold up his own weight. I was beginning to understand what Joe had meant when he had explained dyadic therapy to me. My terrifying childhood memories were slowly being over written, just like old files on a computer hard drive.

Dad had rushed to the hotel ahead of me. He'd gone in and paid for my accommodation and was trying to leave before I got there. Apparently, he had taken the hint after all. In his rush back to the car he had tripped and fallen into the carpark gate, hitting the side of his head. I pulled the car over getting out as quickly as I could. Dad looked up at me, clearly embarrassed, "Well that wasn't quite the impression I wanted to make," he chuckled, blood flowing freely from a gash in his head. Someone from the hotel was already administering first aid, and I waited until he was on his feet again. Refusing further offers of help from the hotel staff he took his keys out of his pocket. "Does the invitation to dinner still stand?" he asked tentatively.

"Sure Dad," I said. "Do you need us to drive you home or something?"

"Na, all good, heads always bleed like a stuck pig," he said, "See you at six at the RSL club," and then he drove away.

Ricky and I spent the next couple of days doing the touristy thing. Once I thought I could handle it, I began doing the things I came to Townsville for. I started off small and called by my old school in Aitkenvale. A large fence encapsulated it now, but I was delighted that the old Moreton Bay fig trees I'd loved to play in as a little girl still stood. I decided I'd drive from there to my old house. I wanted to see how far it really was that I used to walk. I remembered the route easily and didn't need the navigator. It turned out to be about 2.5km, but may have been a little shorter when we were kids. Many of the subdivisions hadn't been built yet, so cutting through the bush and paddocks was our usual route. As a kid it had felt much further, but shorter legs take more steps.

Pulling up in front of my old house was a little more confronting. Once shiny and new, it looked old and dated. The beautiful big tree my sisters and I had planted in the front yard stood dead. Its crumbling old branches looked like they might drop at any minute. No longer a home for noisy rainbow lorikeets who'd feast on the flowers in the late afternoon. My sisters and I would sit cross-legged at the window laughing together at the bird's silly antics, not knowing where our parents were. I closed my eyes and could hear my sisters giggling travelling through time. Some things had been happy here, I remembered.

Feeling the shift in me, Ricky checked in, "You okay?" he asked. "Make sure you stay with me," fully aware of the potential this moment had for me to disassociate. I nodded in acknowledgement but couldn't take my eyes away from the house.

What struck me was how low it was. In my memories it seemed much higher. Whilst I knew it was high set like a lot of homes in the tropics, only 13 steps went from the bottom to the top. I had been so certain it had been at least 30. The awful beige louvers were still below the windows and I recalled all the Saturday mornings I'd spent washing them by hand and hoping they'd pass muster. The small window on the side of the house, now had a security screen over it, but I knew behind it was the kitchen that I got trapped in for hours when

I was 10. I hadn't washed the dishes well enough, and my dad started smashing them on the floor. I jammed myself between the cupboard and the oven to avoid the flying plates. After his fury had ended, he left, leaving me barefoot and unable to make my way to the door. As I sat taking in the sight of my childhood home, I began wondering if I'd be able to do this. Could I really talk to my dad about these things and if I did, would I even get the answers I came for? I began feeling the discomfort from my past pushing into my present, so I called it a day and went back to the temporary sanctuary of my hotel room.

-THE 500-

Dad, Ricky, and I had been meeting for dinner each night around six at Townsville RSL club. It had gotten to our fourth night, and I could see Dad was on edge. He was clearly sick of the small talk, and he still had no idea of why I was in Townsville, so he must have decided to rip the band aid off. Our meals were barely finished when he said very abruptly, "I want to show you something."

He stood bolt upright, a stern and serious look on his face nodding towards another part of the RSL. The front of his thighs grazed the edge of the table as he stood, sending what was left of his beer splashing back and forth in the glass. I noticed he had drunk more that night than he had at our other three dinners, so all sorts of alarm bells started ringing. I immediately looked at Ricky, who had stood when Dad did. He shrugged his shoulders and gave me his *I don't have a clue* look, and they both made their way out of the dining room. I really had no idea what he was about to show or tell me, and I was terrified. I'd come back to Townsville to rewrite my story, to claim my womanhood, to stand up to my father, to say all the things I had never had a chance to. I sensed the moment had presented itself and I just sat there looking at Dad's beer slowly coming to rest. Panic was rapidly rising, and I was paralysed with fear.

I sat there, alone in the dining room. The smell of stale beer floated up my nose and a thousand memories began swirling in my head all at once. The sound of plates being placed on tables was so loud it hurt my ears. Clinking cutlery brought back memories of so many family meals that did not end well. I felt sick. My heart was beating so hard I thought it might push through my chest. I could hear the bells and music of poker machines, eating money and ruining lives. I could hear every conversation happening in the club like the bionic man I'd watched as a kid with supersonic hearing. It felt like everyone was staring at me. I needed to get it together, and fast. I'd waited over 30 years for this moment, and it was galloping away from me. PTSD had taken so many moments from my life. It had pushed and pulled me around for what felt like forever. This was my chance to change all that. I was not going to let it rob me anymore. Taking a deep breath, I reminded myself of why I was here and what adult Christina wanted to do. I was not a little girl anymore. I was the writer of my own story, the healer of my own life. I could walk away if I wanted to. I could do whatever I liked. I choose to heal.

It felt like an hour had passed before Ricky came back and asked if I was coming. My vocal cords were completely constricted. It felt like my throat was going to close in. I only had enough voice to say a tiny yes and stood slowly behind the table. On shaking legs, I followed Ricky into an open lounge bar. I saw my dad standing in front of a wall of framed yellowing newspaper pages. Above the framed pages was a sign simply stating, The 500. Looking at his hunched shoulders and small frame standing in front of the wall, I could see the weight of what he was carrying as he swayed lightly. As I walked closer to him, the faces of young soldiers on the pages came into my awareness. I looked over his hunched shoulders and into the eyes of 500 lost sons. My fear was traded for sadness as I realised these young men were the soldiers lost in Vietnam. A war no one cared about. A political pissing contest that started before I was born and would have enduring impacts on my family for three generations. I began aiming my anger, hurt, and anguish at the government and away from my father. It was the first time I had thought about my dad as a 19-year-old being asked to do things that no one ever should. It was the first time I saw him as a person. It's so easy to forget that our parents are people too. When I approached him, he almost jumped out of his skin. I knew the feeling well when you are lost in the past and get wrenched back before you are ready. We stood side by side looking at the wall not saying a word. Ricky had discreetly moved away but I could see he was not letting me out of his sight.

After what felt like an eternity Dad dropped his head and said in a tiny voice, "Do you know what this is?" All the noises of the RSL club that had been filling my senses earlier faded into the distance as Dad, and what he was about to say, became my only focus.

"No Dad, I don't. Would you like to tell me about it?" I replied.

My dad had never discussed Vietnam with us. He barely even spoke about what he did as a soldier in peacetime so I could feel in my bones that this was going to be an especially important conversation for the both of us. I just hoped like hell I had the courage to have it.

"This is The 500," he said. "The soldiers we lost in Vietnam. We know there are more of them now but when this newspaper came out there were only 500."

I gently reached out for his hand, and he did not pull away. Taking a deep breath and finding calm I asked, "How many of them did you know, Dad?"

From the corner of my eye, I could see a single tear drop from his eyelash and tumble down his bearded face. He inhaled deeply and suddenly stood to attention growing three inches in the process. He gently released my hand and saluting the board, he quietly said, "14."

We spent the next couple of hours talking at the RSL. He shared with me his experiences of war. The great loss of young lives taken by both the enemy and their own hands, to escape the unimaginable horrors of war trauma and PTSD. He told of what it was like to return home to a country enraged by that war. He spoke of having to deal with people who focused their anger on broken teenagers and not the Government who had sent them. Child soldiers whose birthdays were drawn from a lottery ball. Boys who should have been taking girls to dances and singing to Beatles' songs, not hanging out of helicopters shooting strangers they had no beef with. They were too young to even drink at the pub. But at 19 years of age my dad thought he was doing his patriotic duty. Likely inspired by our countries continued glorification of war. Instead, he was labelled a baby killer. He was spat on and had his car vandalised. He spoke of his complete and utter terror of being caught up in the Tet Offensive, unarmed and waiting to end a tour in Saigon. With each disclosure I could see small moments of relief. I could see it was important to him that I knew these stories, that I understood what happened to him.

Suddenly the flow of storytelling stopped. A shameful look passed over his face as he swallowed hard, instinctively checking around him before continuing. The RSL that had sounded so loud before felt like it no longer existed as I was completely consumed by what was unfolding between us.

"There's one last story I really need to tell you," he said, looking at his feet.

I felt a shift in energy between us which I really have no words to describe. I somehow knew this was what I'd come here for and told him to go ahead. He began telling me about the end of his first tour of Vietnam. He told me about arriving home in Sydney and being greeted by his girlfriend at the time. After they had spent the night together, he had fallen asleep with his machete by the bed. He woke in the night after hearing a noise and grabbed for his machete. He saw a small figure in the shadows and ambushed it, holding the machete to their throat.

As he told the story he squeezed his eyes shut; the horror of the moment written on his face. I recognised the story immediately and understood what he was trying to do. The pain of holding a machete to his nine-year-old daughter's throat was too difficult to vocalise, so he had swapped me for a girlfriend and the story continued. He told me his roommate had screamed out his name before he made the final pass of the blade, shaking him from his moment of dissociative flash back.

"I really frightened her," he said. "And for that, I'm so sorry."

He lifted his head and faced me, both of us standing toe to toe, 500 witnesses looking down from the wall. His eyes filled with tears as he explained how he thought he had been back in Vietnam and his 'girlfriend' had been the Viet Cong. "It was a terrible thing to do," he said, "And I never got over it."

We all have choice points in our lives, when we make a decision that changes how you're going to show up in your life going forward and this was one of mine. I had every right to call bullshit on his story and claim it as my own. Having a machete held to my throat by my dad and realising I could have died if my mother hadn't yelled out at exactly the right moment has been a very difficult event to come to terms with. I have lived with its impacts my entire life.

It was hard to listen to my story when it was guest starring someone else. So, I had to decide. Did I want to be right, or did I want to have peace and healing? Standing in my power as a fully grown woman, I could have torn this sick, old man in front of me to pieces. Many might say that he deserved it, and he probably did. If I had gone down that path though, the only thing I would have achieved was to turn myself into the type of person I'd dedicated my whole life not to be. I had offered my mother grace, and he deserved no less. Instead, I reached out to him and pulled him into my arms. We had both been in a war long enough.

I whispered in his ear, "Dad, I am so sorry you've had to go through these things in your life. It must have been so hard for you."

He completely fell to pieces in my arms. He wrapped his hands around my neck and buried his face in my shoulder, crying until my shirt was wet with his tears; crying until he could barely stand on his own. When he finished crying, he looked deeply into my face and said, "I don't deserve your forgiveness, I don't deserve any of this."

I smiled at him and said, "But I do." I could tell by the look on his face that he understood.

Coming from a place of love and compassion came even more easily for me after that day. I saw Dad as a person who had gone through some hellish things. He wasn't perfect and he wasn't the Dad I would have picked. But he was not the monster I had created in my head either. The stories fed to me by my mother to keep me loyal to her and my own childhood memories, began to unravel and released me from my pain and fear.

His war experiences were not an excuse for what happened to my sisters and me, but I could see his actions had also harmed him. He had paid with his mind, body and spirit and it was important to me to try and understand his story so I could understand my own. When I saw him for what he was, a man broken by war and military service, I understood that what had happened in our family was not because of me. I was not a bad child, I hadn't been a terrible daughter, I did none of what I'd been accused of. I was just a little girl with parents who could not cope in the world and had never sought help for the problems they faced. I was surrounded by adults who chose silence over seeing. People who turned the other cheek and did nothing to help three little girls. My anger moved to where it deserved to be, to the systems that created the problems in the first place. Forgiving my dad was incredibly freeing for me. If I can forgive the man who held a machete to my throat, who beat me and my mother and hurt my sisters, then it puts all other things into perspective. Getting cut off in traffic makes you a little less angry after forgiveness like that.

A few days later we would say goodbye to each other at Townsville airport. Now it was my turn to cry. I wished I had more time. There was still so much to say. This time, he took me into *his* arms and for the first time in my life, I felt safe with him. He kissed me gently on the top of my head and in a whisper said, "I love you short stuff."

Crying more heavily, I replied, "I love you too Dad."

We had gotten three days together being father and daughter. My heart felt whole. I got it. This was the dyadic completion Joe had been talking about months earlier. As the call came for my flight, we had to let each other go, both of us changed by compassion and love. As I ascended the escalator, I looked back over my shoulder for a last wave goodbye, my dad looked a whole lot better than when I had arrived and now that is how I remember him, smiling up at me and waving, tears glistening in his eyes.

We talked a lot on the phone after my trip to Townsville and continued to heal each other through words of truth and unconditional love, but it would be the last time I would see him alive. His soul left this earth around the 19th of March 2020. He died at home in Townsville alone, the system letting him down one last time, discharging him from the Mater Private Hospital without ensuring his care agency knew. A forgotten soldier who did his duty.

Due to COVID-19 restrictions at the time of his death, he was cremated alone at 11am on the 26th of March 2020. Dad never had a funeral or the acknowledgment a soldier who fought for our country should have, but to be honest, I don't think he would have wanted it anyway. His memorial plaque, provided by the Australian Army, is on a wall in *Anzac Memorial Park Townsville* overlooking his beloved Strand and out to Magnetic Island. He is surrounded by other diggers, some of whom made the ultimate sacrifice and others who made it more slowly. He will never be alone again.

-Going Forward-

In the time following Mum and Dad's death, I dove deeper into my healing journey, pulling back each layer I had carefully wrapped myself in to protect my tender heart. After returning from Townsville in 2018, I started seeing my life through a different lens. Whilst I'd never really identified with the title of 'victim' I had still been living under the weight of its limitations without realising it. I had blamed myself for everything that went wrong with our family. If only I had been a better daughter, better sister; if only I had done more, if only I was prettier, smarter, thinner, quicker, talked less, talked more, if only I had been anything other than me. The work with my parents had brought all that thinking to a close but not thinking like that anymore left a gap in my life. I had not let being a victim become my personality, but my upbringing consumed so many of my thoughts and actions I honestly felt very lost without them. My whole lifetime had been about surviving and it felt so strange not to be doing that anymore. I no longer wanted to talk about trauma and sadness or take part in conversations that were almost a 'competitive go around' of who had the harder life as if it was some type of competition; the prize being a lifetime of misery and depression. *Yeah, nah, no thanks.* Instead, I looked forward with happiness and optimism. The only problem? I had started to make the people around me very uncomfortable.

Often when I'd meet up with friends, they'd want to get together and gossip about traumatic or low energy things. "Oh, you got locked in your room for a few hours. I used to get locked in my room for a whole weekend!" they'd cry. "Oh, you think that's bad? At least you had sisters to go through it with – I was an only child."

As they say, like attracts like, and I was in circles that no longer served me. I didn't have it in me anymore to compare traumatic experiences, or try to one-up people, and so, I ended up losing a lot of friendships.

My lack of boundaries and wanting to help and please had attracted certain people to me. As my granny used to say, "Misery loves company" and it did – my low energy had attracted more of the same into my life. Some borrowed money only to dash and I'd never see them or the money again; some would dump all their problems on me but never be there to help me with mine, I'd baby sit kids for free, I loaned my car, tutored and so on, I think you get the picture. When I returned from Townsville, I would not do it anymore and I began saying no. Slowly the 'friends' began falling away until there were none, and I was okay with that. Even today, apart from my immediate family, I have only a few people left in my life from before 2018.

Being essentially friendless for a while was the best gift I could have been given and allowed me the space I needed to explore who I really was, free of the shackles that had kept me connected to my past. I worked with Joe for a couple of years after seeing Dad and then I realised I didn't need that sort of support anymore. I had begun enjoying music again, I took up yoga as an extension of my somatic work, I danced, I ran, I joined a boot camp and got fit and healthy, I was introduced to parkrun by Robb 'Dingo' Blake which got me back out helping in my community again. Life was becoming good, however I struggled to get the balance right.

In life we are always hearing about the holy trinity (not *that* one, the other one) of Mind, Body and Spirit. It was a mental juggle, and I just could not seem to get the balance right no matter how hard I tried. I would focus on my mental health, then drop the body ball, I would focus on my body but drop the mind ball and the spiritual ball only came into play on special occasions. I really loved all the aspects of the trinity and what they had to offer but could never figure out how to bring the three together. Then I met a woman named Rebecca.

Now that I'm back in touch with my spiritual self (don't stress, I'm not going to go *woo woo* on you), I have complete and utter faith in the universe. It will and always has brought me exactly what I need at exactly the time I need it. When I cast my mind back on my life, I can see all the different times that this had happened without me realising it, good or bad, "the universe is unfolding exactly as it should" (Max Ehrmann).

Rebecca Thompson and The Beacons coming into my life were no different. What I didn't know was that she held the final key that would teach me how to bring all that I had learned in my 51 years on earth together into one body; I'd heal the last wounds of my inner child, who I'd gone to such a massive effort to collect from Townsville. I would heal my mother wound more fully allowing me to have women friends that I could be my real self with and trust them with my heart, authentic friendships that will stand the test of time and beyond. I would find joy, love and peace ironically in another RSL, but on Bribie Island this time and then Magnetic Island and Horseshoe Bay a couple of years later. That cyclic nature of life played out for me again, returning me full circle to places I had been before, showing me how far I'd come. Rebecca and The Beacons taught me extremely valuable lessons that gave depth to my healing and brought balance into my life. I would love to share a few of my takeaways with you now.

Surrender

The first time Rebecca talked to me about the concept of surrender, I felt instant resistance. It made me feel angry, annoyed, and almost sick. The fact that I am alive and have the life I have today is because I never once surrendered, and I would not start it now. But that is not what she meant. I could never get the balance right because I was always forcing it. I had never been taught how to surrender, what battles were worth it, what ones weren't and how to tell the difference. I had always had to fight for the most basic things in my life and I was still doing it. I'd make myself read a book right to the end even if I didn't like it; I'd stay in jobs I hated because "I'll never let the bastards beat me." I had the picture of the frog being eaten by the stork, the frogs' hands around the stork's neck with the words, *Never Give Up*, emboldened across the bottom plastered on my notice board. I might not have had a victim mentality, but I certainly had developed a survivor's one. I was so entangled with being a survivor it had permeated every aspect of my life and was making things more difficult than they needed to be. I had to learn how to surrender and go with the flow more. I was obsessively trying to control every aspect of mine and my family's life, and all it did was generate a false sense of security. I was tiring myself out trying to make things happen that were never going to and fighting battles I no longer needed to fight. So, I learned the art of surrender and to let things be what they are going to be. Through surrender I finally learned how to meditate and give my mind the peace it so desperately needed. The practice of yin yoga and meditation soothed my nervous system further and gave me even more chances to learn how to surrender, deepening my somatic work even more. Without manically obsessing over everything it gave me more space to explore teaching again, and I started my own reiki business after becoming qualified as a Reiki Master Teacher. I realised that at my core I am still a teacher, but I let go of what I thought being a teacher had to look like and let the embodiment of what it is to teach come fully into being. Coaching, counselling, and presenting workshops let me share with people what has taken me years to learn, fast tracking their healing journeys. My reiki business morphed into a wholistic counselling and coaching business. I am back helping others again, but this time in an extremely healthy way, without compromising myself. Teaching is my joy, and I welcomed its return

Vulnerability

I used to think that vulnerability was a weakness. That's certainly what I'd been taught, as the daughter of an army sergeant and a little girl surrounded by school yards full of bullies, I was super proud of how strong I was – I rarely cried and felt I could manage every situation life threw at me.

Vulnerability was for the weak – or so I thought. In truth, – I was wrong.

I have never felt more emotionally stronger than when I felt vulnerable for the first time. I had felt it a bit in Joe's office, but I'd never committed to the whole feeling, still viewing it as a weakness. I wish I had a dollar for every time I would start crying in his office, apologise and stop myself. I found being vulnerable one of the hardest things to do.

My trauma had made me hyper-independent, as I had only myself to rely on growing up, but I didn't need to be like that anymore. The hyper-independence created issues for me in the workplace and at home and I honestly could not understand what the problem was until I started working with vulnerability. I began seeing that my lack of vulnerability was impacting how I wanted to show up in the world. My fear of being hurt by someone made me hold everyone at arm's length, close enough to see, but not close enough to feel. I would never ask for help or take it when it was offered and had difficulty trusting anyone who wasn't close to me. I had so much love to give others, but I never let them give it back.

Love had been weaponised in my world; it had been given out conditionally and brutally taken away without notice. I had grown up without any room for vulnerability and it was the hardest of things to learn. To help me understand, I read the *Power of Vulnerability and Rising Strong* by Brené Brown, and she wrote, "Vulnerability is not weakness; it's our greatest measure of courage." I had gotten it all wrong. It took a hell of a lot more courage for me to rock up to Bribie Island RSL with my history, be surrounded by army paraphernalia and be vulnerable with a group of women I had only just met, than it would have taken to stay safely tucked away at home.

By learning to be vulnerable, I opened a new layer to my heart that had been frozen shut for years. I had been selfish with my love of others. I never allowed it to be returned. I had never considered that people might like to love me in the same way I loved them, and I had never considered the hurt I caused by not letting them. Opening the doors of vulnerability has been extremely liberating and being capable of receiving all the love I had always wanted to but had never known repaired not only my spiritual self but many aspects of my physical health too. In my vulnerability I began saying yes to new opportunities which took me into studying counselling. Working with people, especially children, who have experienced trauma is extremely rewarding. Without the power of vulnerability that would not have been possible and has allowed me to feel the full potency of life.

Mindfulness

I know everyone is probably sick and tired of hearing about mindfulness by now, but it really is a powerful tool. I think corporations and institutions have probably ruined the idea a bit by leaping onto it without fully understanding what it is or how to use it. It is being presented as a cheap mental health tool they can roll out and make the employee completely responsible for.

Sarcastic side note: Nice work HR for hijacking an ancient and beautiful practice and getting everyone to hate it!

Mindfulness has been a very tricky process to learn and most people I work with say a similar thing.

For me mindfulness means being fully present in the moment, which is easier said than done. My trauma and PTSD had me always coming up with contingency plans. This way of thinking trapped me in two ways; I was always living in the future, planning for the possible outcome of every scenario my imagination could muster. I could not just enjoy the moment I was in. I had to plan for the pending disaster that I always thought was only moments away and thinking this way had me always *looking* for a pending disaster that I always thought was only moments away.

Living in my survival brain all the time was an exhausting experience, but when your life depends on it, being able to spot a potential threat before everyone else is a useful skill indeed. It helped so many times they are too numerous to mention. My survival brain had served me well, but it was now robbing me of fun and joy, I didn't need it anymore. I would go to a park with my family and rather than join in the fun I would be patrolling like a bouncer on a Saturday night in Fortitude Valley, ever vigilant for the threat that never came. I recall a weekend snorkeling trip I took with some fellow teachers that I never participated in, as I stayed watch, convinced someone would either drown or be eaten by a shark- in a rock pool. Even all these years later, I still feel quite sad thinking about all that I have missed out on whilst planning for disasters that have never happened. Have you ever been driving your car and then suddenly realized you were somewhere down the road but couldn't remember how you got there? Then you need to learn some mindfulness. Our hectic fast-paced lives have us chasing the next thing and the thing after that, overlooking the joy of the moment we are in. We don't stop to celebrate our successes or commiserate our losses; we are always thinking about tomorrow, a mystical land that never comes.

After I lost my brother-in-law Andy, I began to understand the importance of each moment we have and with The Beacons, I fully embraced the ideas of mindfulness. I started small at first, being mindful in the way I drove my car – the feeling of my bottom on the seat, the cool air conditioning blowing on my face, the bumps of the car as it rolled along the highway, how the steering wheel would feel in my hand. Every time my mind would move to accidents or sink holes, I'd gently and without judgment, bring my focus back to the car, my driving it and how it was to exist just in that moment. I still plan for things, I need to do that too, but I also do that mindfully and with purpose. Now when I am enjoying something like a concert or a meal, a walk in the rainforest or music on the radio, I use my whole body to be present in the moment. If I feel something come up for me, I allow it to and then I let it fade away without having to attach a story to it or chase the feeling down an endless maze of rabbit holes. Part of being mindful has included putting my phone away, especially when I am with loved ones- smart phones are the natural enemy of mindfulness and I am never properly present if I have one on me. Being properly present in my life has given me immense joy and I live now in a brighter more colorful way, free of the pressures that come with living constantly in the future.

<u>Loving Myself</u>

Loving myself exactly as I am has been hard. I know this is not unique to me and nearly everyone I know – especially women born in the '60s and '70s, can really struggle with loving themselves. Every time I'd entertain it, I'd hear the schoolyard bullies chanting, "You love yourself Christina, you're so up yourself!" Or I'd hear my mother say, "Don't go out in the wind, your tickets will blow off." People who find it hard to love themselves seem to want to stop other people from doing it. I will never understand why. Before I got serious about healing, I found it hard to do the most basic things to love myself. I would feel guilty if I did the slightest thing that might bring me joy and that only worsened when I became a mother. Intent on being the opposite to my mum, I went way too far with it, denying myself new underwear, haircuts or shoes in the earnest belief it was taking away from my children. I famously got married wearing a pair of undies that my husband had tried to throw out on multiple occasions – not the sexy surprise I'm sure he was hoping for on our wedding night. I've kept them with my wedding dress, first as a joke but now as a reminder not to go there again. I achieved nothing in denying myself and was modeling some horrible life skills to my children, especially my daughter. Whilst I was meeting their every need physically, emotionally, I was letting them down, and I needed to lift my game. Denying myself was not making me a better mother or person, it was just feeding into an old story of not being worthy of anything.

When I first started exploring ideas of self-love, an image of me standing in front of my bathroom mirror wearing hideously thick make up and blowing myself little kisses appeared in my mind's eye. But that's not it. When I understood what self-love was and looked like, it became easier. I was so used to only seeing value in myself through what I could do for others, so doing things for myself felt like a wasted effort.

Like all new processes I started off small, booking haircuts more often than once a year, I got a facial and I was 51 years old before I had my first massage. I started to tend to my doctor's appointments with more consistency. I thought what it might be like to tell my loved ones I might die because I did not think that I was worthy of a pap smear or a breast screen. Can you imagine? I ate healthier, said no to things that I would usually do out of obligation and then the love became more internalised.

At a retreat Rebecca was hosting, we were doing mother wound work and part of that was saying the Hooponopono Prayer. It simply says, "I'm sorry, please forgive me, thank you, I love you." We repeated it several times to a proxy who represented our mothers, and they said it back to us. Standing in the powerful presence of unconditional love is hard to put into words. I had offered it so many times to others but never to myself. On that day, I felt a shift in me. I did go to the mirror after that, but it was not a clown-like caricature of myself I saw like the visions I conjured up around self-love. It was a strong, beautiful woman, and I loved myself. I had forgiven everyone around me, but I had never forgiven myself. I hadn't even realised I needed to. Self-love led me to love myself exactly as I am. I stopped trying to be who I thought other people wanted me to be and finally felt comfortable in my own skin. Exploring self-love also unlocked another part of my puzzle, leading me to receive a late life diagnosis of Attention Deficit Hyperactivity Disorder and Autism Spectrum Disorder, which I'll explore in a future book.

My healing and growth are still ongoing and probably always will be, but I approach it now with my heart wide open and a willingness that was missing in my younger self.

I once had someone say to me, "You've no right to the sanity you have." I was really offended by it at first until I realised what they were trying to say was they could not understand, after all I'd endured, that I could still approach my life the way that I do. My experiences had not left me feeling jaded, angry or bitter. I did not become a statistic. I explained that over the years I did get angry, I am only human after all, but I found anger never got me anywhere. Neither did hate or trying to be cruel. I had tried all those things on and found they never fit. Buddha reportedly said hatred is like drinking poison and expecting the other person to die. I really get that. But what the person said got me curious about myself. Having spent many years teaching, one thing I did know was troubled, abused, and neglected kids like I had been, frequently did not have great outcomes. They'd often end up violent, struggling with addiction and eventually in the system, but I hadn't. I wondered what it was that had helped me avoid a similar fate.

I once asked Joe if he knew why I hadn't been lost to anger and hate, and he shared that he thought it was because of love.

Love had made my life the way it was possible. Even in the middle of the chaos I was still able to connect myself to love. First it was the love of my little sisters. Loving them and keeping them safe had helped me connect to something outside of myself and helped me stay in touch with my humanity; loving animals taught me the rewards and benefits that came with being gentle and kind and how good that felt; loving my students helped me refocus my trauma and my pain, making it mean something in the hope I could make things better for others because of it; loving my husband and my kids made me determined not to pass on the trauma that my parents had given me. I often reflect on *What Love Made Possible* and what my life might be like without it.

I explained to the person who had asked about my sanity that it was never about what the other people did, it was about the type of person **I** wanted to be. No matter what has happened in my life I always get to choose how I want to be. I decide how I want to show up in my life, and no one can ever take that from me.

Healing like this is an ugly business and do not let any crazy person selling snake oil on the internet tell you otherwise. It is hard and you must be brave to do it. It is not for the faint of heart and it will push you and pull you until you feel like you are going crazy in a different way than you were before. That's the honest to god truth of it, in my experience anyway. Healing like I have done had me facing my darkest fears and taking responsibility for my own life. It would have been easy for me to stay cocooned in trauma and blame my parents and when you hear my story you would not have been surprised if I did, but I owed the little girl in me a chance to live the life she dreamt of. A big, beautiful life full of love, learning and laughter, and I was not going to settle for anything less.

And never will.

Afterword

-Thoughts on Love and Hope-

The world often feels like a harsh and difficult place to live in and that's never been truer than it is today. So many global events flashing through the devices in the palms of our hands signalling a permanent SOS to our nervous systems. We are constantly sold to and talked at to the point where we are beginning to lose our humanity and if the past is any indicator of the future, when we lose our humanity terrible things start to happen. I have found myself asking, *But is it true?*

Is the world really this bad or have we subscribed to a false narrative designed to fuel capitalism and hate? Systems created to elevate those in power, enslaving the rest of us through fear and division – when we have fully turned on each other we can't hold those we should to account for failing in their duties to society. Governments, corporations, education systems, churches and councils – bloated bureaucratic systems constantly thriving from the repression and misery of others. When my focus began to fall on those it should, it freed my heart to see those around me in different ways and act from a place of compassion, empathy, and love.

I began wondering what the world would look like if we could see each other as humans with failings and flaws, but still united in our common goal to live happy lives. What if we could just be satisfied with having enough to meet our needs? Clothing, food, a roof over our heads… You don't realise the simple pleasures of these things until you haven't had them and I've been there.

I've survived poverty and violence, abuse and sometimes torture. Being conceived out of wedlock in the late 1960s and spending most of the rest of my life being told how I had ruined my mother's by my very existence. Raised by two parents, with mental health issues and problems with addiction in a time where it was impolite to interfere with other people's families and adults didn't believe children no matter what you said or how you said it. Children were to be seen and not heard, silent citizens sent to the shop with notes to buy their parents alcohol or cigarettes, and if you were lucky you got to keep the change. When bad things happened to you no one wanted to hear about it. You just smiled and got on with it, the damage surfacing later in the form of anxiety, depression, complex PTSD, trauma, health issues and the list goes on.

If my sisters and I had been children today and adults knew our story we most likely would have been raised in the foster care system and I don't know if that would have been a good thing or not. Depending on our luck, I may or may not still be writing this story today.

I find it fascinating that a decision I made when I was eight years old to always choose love and hope, would go on to shape my life, be a driving force for positive change, introduce me to my husband and impact so many people around me. Whilst my idea to teach began as a way to emulate the adults that made me feel safe, ultimately the path to becoming a teacher created structure and stability in my life where there was none, it gave me a goal and dream to aim for. Wanting to be a teacher gave me hope that my life might be different one day. That hope helped me keep going. It ultimately helped me survive.

What are we if we don't have hope and love?

-About the Author-

Photo Credit: Mel Watt Photography

Christina Graham is an award-winning businesswoman, mentor, and passionate advocate for mental health awareness and inclusive education. With 22 years of teaching experience across early childhood, primary, and tertiary education — including at the *University of Southern Queensland* — she works closely with families to ensure children with complex needs receive the education and support they deserve.

As the founder of *Heart-to-Heart Conversations*, Christina draws on her deep compassion, lived experience of trauma, and expertise in neurodivergence to help others create the lives they dream of. She is a sought-after mentor and presenter, known for her ability to connect with people in meaningful, transformative ways.

In 2026, Christina released her debut book, *What Love Made Possible* — a moving and courageous account of breaking the cycle of intergenerational trauma and discovering true healing.

Christina lives in Queensland with her husband of 30 years, Ricky, and treasures time with her children and grandchildren. When she isn't writing, teaching, or presenting, she can be found enjoying nature or cherishing quiet moments with her beloved animals.

–Work With Me–

If you're seeking a compelling and heartfelt speaker to inspire your audience on topics such as **overcoming adversity, inclusivity, the transformative power of education, neurodiversity in schools and workplaces**, or **the enduring strength of hope**, I'd love to connect. I speak from lived experience—sharing stories that are raw, real, and ultimately empowering.

My **presentations are engaging, relatable, and deeply human**. Whether speaking to educators, parents, corporate teams, or community groups, I aim to create safe spaces for honest conversations that challenge, uplift, and inspire. I draw on both personal insights and professional expertise to deliver messages that resonate long after the session ends. Participants often describe my talks as "eye-opening," "encouraging," and "exactly what we needed to hear."

My coaching practice blends the insights gained from my personal journey with over two decades in education and mentoring. I support individuals, families, and organisations through a **collaborative, client-centred approach**, underpinned by **authentic presence, compassionate listening**, and a deep respect for each person's path. Sessions are thoughtfully tailored to meet each client's unique needs, offering both emotional support and practical strategies for growth and change.

To book Christina as a speaker, discuss a workshop or to enquire about private one on one sessions, reach out at www.hearttoheartconversations.com.au

Connect with Christina Graham

🌐 *www.hearttoheartconversations.com.au*

🌐 *https://www.christinagrahambooks.com/*

📘 *https://www.facebook.com/hearttoheartconversations*

📘 *https://www.facebook.com/christinagrahamauthor/*

-Acknowledgments (Angel People)-

<u>Joseph Riordan (psychologist):</u>
Thank you for taking this journey with me when others wouldn't and for your unwavering patience and care. I admire that you were brave enough to try and find another way to help people outside of traditional methods; you have fought the good fight for people like me and your influence will span generations through your work and writing, including the paper that has my family in it.

<u>Rebecca Thompson (mentor and spiritual teacher):</u>
I'm so grateful to you for creating The Beacons and for the work you continue to do. You walk the talk and are a great source of inspiration to those who know you. Thank you for being the grit for my pearl to grow and for being the first to really see me. I hope all I learned from you will help me to help others. You helped me learn how to live with 'my heart wide open'.

https://www.beksthompson.com/

The Beacons (including Rebecca):

I love every one of you women with all my heart and soul. Thank you for showing me that life is best lived when it's shared with friends. To The Beacon Angels Jodie W, Wendy, Gemma, and Patty I appreciate all you have done for me, especially when I wasn't in my finest of moments. I carry you all with me in all I say and do.

Jas Rawlinson:

As my book coach and mentor, I know without you this book would be still sitting in my head. I appreciate all you did for me to get this over the line. You believed in my story from the very start; you were the first to read it and the first to congratulate me when it was done. Your cheerleading means more than you will ever know. I'm so very glad to know you and I'm so proud of the work you do in the advocacy space of protecting women and children and raising awareness around domestic and family violence

https://www.jasrawlinson.com/

Vietnam Veterans and Their Families:

I want to acknowledge other Veterans and their families, many of whom have stories not dissimilar to mine. I'm so sorry that war came and impacted so many of our families. I want you to know I was thinking of you all too whilst I was writing this book and I hope peace and joy have found you, if not already, someday soon. I would especially like to acknowledge 'The 500' and more young men who lost their lives in the Vietnam War. My dad felt the loss of every last one of you for the rest of his days.

Townsville RSL:

Thank you for giving my dad a place to go and a place to be, even when he wasn't always on his best behaviour. I appreciate you looking out for him. Your RSL gave us a place to reconnect and for me to finally understand what my dad faced as an Australian Soldier.

Phil 'Sparra' and Anne Newey:

Thanks so much for wandering into my little shop and taking the time to talk to me and encourage me to see Joe – it changed my life. Thank you Phil for providing me a different point of view around Vietnam Veterans. You were the first soldier I wasn't afraid of.

Rhys and Leanne Lucinsky:

Whilst I didn't get the chance to mention you directly in my book, I would still like to acknowledge your incredible kindness of standing in a dusty old carpark in Bloomsbury North Queensland where I stopped at 11 am March 26th, 2020, to commemorate my dad being cremated. I was alone and heading back to Brisbane during the first lockdowns. Even though your travelling karaoke business had just come to a sudden close, you put that to one side and invited this strange, weird crying lady over to your caravan for a cup of tea. Not having to be alone whilst the last post was being played on my iPhone meant the world to me and I've never forgotten it. In a time of great grief, being my angels when I needed it was really appreciated. Wishing many successes to *Wander'n Star Karaoke.*

https://www.facebook.com/profile.php?id=100051709489307

Townsville Funerals, Cremations and Crematorium:

I'd like to thank and acknowledge the gorgeous owners and staff at Townsville Crematorium. You helped me navigate a really weird time in history – losing a family member right at the start of a global pandemic. You helped me deal with the police, gave me PPE when it was sold out everywhere and you checked out my dad's flat for me to make sure it was okay for me to enter and clean out as he had been passed away in there for a couple of weeks. You went above and beyond for me and my family, and I have never forgotten it.

https://www.townsvillecremations.com.au/

Scott Radford- Chisholm:

A professional photographer in Townsville. Thank you for answering our call on a local *Facebook* page and photographing Dad's memorial plate in Townsville, during the pandemic and sending me the pictures. It took a couple of years to see it in person, so your pictures were really precious to us and we appreciate your generosity of your time to take them and send them to us.

https://www.srcphotos.com.au/index

-Recommended Reading-

Brown, B. (2017). *Braving the wilderness: The quest for true belonging and the courage to stand alone*. Random House.

Brown, B. (2015). *Daring greatly: How the courage to be vulnerable transforms the way we live, love, parent, and lead*. Penguin.

Brown, B. (2015). *Rising strong*. Random House.

Brown, B. (2022). *The gifts of imperfection: Let go of who you think you're supposed to be and embrace who you are*. Simon and Schuster.

Ehrmann, M. (2017). *The desiderata of happiness*. Souvenir Press.

Hari, J. (2018). *Lost connections: Uncovering the real causes of depression-and the unexpected solutions*. London: Bloomsbury Circus.

LePera, D. N. (2021). *How to Do the Work*. Harper Wave.

Levine, P. A. (1997). *Waking the tiger: Healing trauma: The innate capacity to transform overwhelming experiences.* North Atlantic Books.

Levine, P. A. (2010). In an unspoken voice: How the body releases trauma and restores goodness. *North Atlantic Books.*

Riordan, J. P., Blakeslee, A., & Levine, P. (2019). Attachment focused-somatic experiencing®: Secure phylogenetic attachment, dyadic trauma and completion across the life cycle. *International Journal of Neuropsychotherapy, 7*(3), 57-90.

Riordan, J. (2024). Attachment traumatology and dyadic completion: Toddler trauma, ten years post-treatment. *Journal of Applied Neurosciences, 3*(1). https://doi.org/10.4102/jan.v3i1.15

Riordan, J. P. (2022). Dyadic trauma and attachment: A monozygotic twin study assessing the efficacy of Somatic Experiencing®. *Journal of Applied Neurosciences, 1*(1), 3.

Riordan, J. P. (2023). Attachment Traumatology: Interpersonal neurosynchronistic phylogenesis. *Journal of Applied Neurosciences, 2*(1). https://doi.org/10.4102/jan.v2i1.7

Van Der Kolk, B. (2015). The body keeps the score. Penguin Books.

-Notes-